THE WORKS OF
HERMAN MELVILLE

STANDARD EDITION

VOLUME

XIV

CLAREL

A POEM AND PILGRIMAGE IN THE HOLY LAND

BY

HERMAN MELVILLE

IN TWO VOLUMES

VOL. I

NEW YORK

RUSSELL & RUSSELL · INC

1963

THE STANDARD EDITION OF

THE WORKS OF HERMAN MELVILLE

IN SIXTEEN VOLUMES

REISSUED, 1963, BY RUSSELL & RUSSELL, INC.

L. C. CATALOG CARD NO: 63–18862

PRINTED IN THE UNITED STATES OF AMERICA

CLAREL was first published in 1876 (New York: G. P. Putnam's Sons) No English edition was ever issued. The first edition contained the following author's note :—
' If during the period in which this work has remained unpublished, though not undivulged, any of its properties have by a natural process exhaled ; it yet retains, I trust, enough of original life to redeem it at least from vapidity. Be that as it may, I here dismiss the book—content beforehand with whatever future awaits it.'

BY A SPONTANEOUS ACT, NOT VERY LONG AGO

MY KINSMAN, THE LATE

PETER GANSEVOORT

OF ALBANY, N.Y.

IN A PERSONAL INTERVIEW PROVIDED FOR
THE PUBLICATION OF THIS POEM, KNOWN TO
HIM BY REPORT, AS EXISTING IN MANUSCRIPT

JUSTLY AND AFFECTIONATELY THE PRINTED
BOOK IS INSCRIBED WITH HIS NAME

CONTENTS

PART I

JERUSALEM

		PAGE
I.	THE HOSTEL	3
II.	ABDON	9
III.	THE SEPULCHRE	14
IV.	OF THE CRUSADERS	20
V.	CLAREL	22
VI.	TRIBES AND SECTS	29
VII.	BEYOND THE WALLS	31
VIII.	THE VOTARY	34
IX.	SAINT AND STUDENT	37
X.	RAMBLES	39
XI.	LOWER GIHON	43
XII.	CELIO	46
XIII.	THE ARCH	51
XIV.	IN THE GLEN	55
XV.	UNDER THE MINARET	60
XVI.	THE WALL OF WAIL	63
XVII.	NATHAN	69
XVIII.	NIGHT	80

b

PAGE

XIX. THE FULFILMENT 84

XX. VALE OF ASHES 86

XXI. BY-PLACES 88

XXII. HERMITAGE 90

XXIII. THE CLOSE 94

XXIV. THE GIBE 97

XXV. HUTS 100

XXVI. THE GATE OF ZION 103

XXVII. MATRON AND MAID 106

XXVIII. TOMB AND FOUNTAIN 110

XXIX. THE RECLUSE 115

XXX. THE SITE OF THE PASSION 117

XXXI. ROLFE 121

XXXII. OF RAMA 130

XXXIII. BY THE STONE 132

XXXIV. THEY TARRY 136

XXXV. ARCULF AND ADAMNAN 139

XXXVI. THE TOWER 143

XXXVII. A SKETCH 146

XXXVIII. THE SPARROW 150

XXXIX. CLAREL AND RUTH 152

XL. THE MOUNDS 154

XLI. ON THE WALL 157

XLII. TIDINGS 162

XLIII. A PROCESSION 165

XLIV. THE START 167

CONTENTS

PART II

THE WILDERNESS

		PAGE
I.	THE CAVALCADE	171
II.	THE SKULL-CAP	179
III.	BY THE GARDEN	181
IV.	OF MORTMAIN	187
V.	CLAREL AND GLAUCON	192
VI.	THE HAMLET	195
VII.	GUIDE AND GUARD	197
VIII.	ROLFE AND DERWENT	201
IX.	THROUGH ADOMMIN	203
X.	A HALT	207
XI.	OF DESERTS	215
XII.	THE BANKER	218
XIII.	FLIGHT OF THE GREEKS	221
XIV.	BY ACHOR	226
XV.	THE FOUNTAIN	230
XVI.	NIGHT IN JERICHO	233
XVII.	IN MID-WATCH	238
XVIII.	THE SYRIAN MONK	240
XIX.	AN APOSTATE	245
XX.	UNDER THE MOUNTAIN	248
XXI.	THE PRIEST AND ROLFE	252
XXII.	CONCERNING HEBREWS	257

PAGE

XXIII. BY THE JORDAN 262

XXIV. THE RIVER-RITE 268

XXV. THE DOMINICAN 271

XXVI. OF ROME 278

XXVII. VINE AND CLAREL 284

XXVIII. THE FOG 290

XXIX. BY THE MARGE 292

XXX. OF PETRA 298

XXXI. THE INSCRIPTION 301

XXXII. THE ENCAMPMENT 305

XXXIII. LOT'S SEA 309

XXXIV. MORTMAIN REAPPEARS 313

XXXV. PRELUSIVE 316

XXXVI. SODOM 318

XXXVII. OF TRADITIONS 322

XXXVIII. THE SLEEP-WALKER 325

XXXIX. OBSEQUIES 327

PART I
JERUSALEM

A

I

In chamber low and scored by time,
Masonry old, late washed with lime—
Much like a tomb new-cut in stone ;
Elbow on knee, and brow sustained
All motionless on sidelong hand,
A student sits, and broods alone.
The small deep casement sheds a ray
Which tells that in the Holy Town
It is the passing of the day—
The Vigil of Epiphany.
Beside him in the narrow cell
His luggage lies unpacked ; thereon
The dust lies, and on him as well—
The dust of travel.   But anon
His face he lifts—in feature fine,
Yet pale, and all but feminine
But for the eye and serious brow—
Then rises, paces to and fro,
And pauses, saying, ' Other cheer
Than that anticipated here,
By me the learner, now I find.
Theology, art thou so blind ?
What means this naturalistic knell
In lieu of Siloh's oracle
Which here should murmur ?   Snatched
    from grace,
And waylaid in the holy place !

Not thus it was but yesterday
Off Jaffa on the clear blue sea ;
Nor thus, my heart, it was with thee
Landing amid the shouts and spray ;
Nor thus when mounted, full equipped,
Out through the vaulted gate we slipped
Beyond the walls where gardens bright
With bloom and blossom cheered the sight.
The plain we crossed.   In afternoon,
How like our early autumn bland—
So softly tempered for a boon—
The breath of Sharon's prairie land !
And was it, yes, her titled Rose,
That scarlet poppy oft at hand ?
Then Ramleh gleamed, the sail-white town
At even.   There I watched day close
From the fair tower, the suburb one :
Seaward and dazing set the sun :
Inland I turned me toward the wall
Of Ephraim, stretched in purple pall.
Romance of mountains !   But in end
What change the near approach could lend.
     ' The start this morning—gun and lance
Against the quarter-moon's low tide ;
The thieves' huts where we hushed the ride ;
Chill day-break in the lorn advance ;
In stony strait the scorch of noon,
Thrown off by crags, reminding one
Of those hot paynims whose fierce hands
Flung showers of Afric's fiery sands
In face of that crusader-king,
Louis, to wither so his wing ;
And, at the last, aloft for goal,
Like the ice-bastions round the Pole,
Thy blank, blank towers, Jerusalem ! '

Again he droops, with brow on hand.
But, starting up, ' Why, well I knew
Salem to be no Samarcand ;
'Twas scarce surprise ; and yet first view
Brings this eclipse.   Needs be my soul,
Purged by the desert's subtle air
From bookish vapours, now is heir
To nature's influx of control ;
Comes likewise now to consciousness
Of the true import of that press
Of inklings which in travel late
Through Latin lands, did vex my state,
And somehow seemed clandestine.   Ah !
These under-formings in the mind.
Banked corals which ascend from far,
But little heed men that they wind
Unseen, unheard—till lo, the reef—
The reef and breaker, wreck and grief.
But here unlearning, how to me
Opes the expanse of time's vast sea !
Yes, I am young, but Asia old.
The books, the books not all have told.
    ' And, for the rest, the facile chat
Of overweenings—what was that
The grave one said in Jaffa lane
Whom there I met, my countryman,
But new-returned from travel here ;
Some word of mine provoked the strain ;
His meaning now begins to clear :
Let me go over it again :—
    ' Our New World's worldly wit so shrewd
Lacks the Semitic reverent mood,
Unworldly—hardly may confer
Fitness for just interpreter
Of Palestine.   Forgo the state

Of local minds inveterate,
Tied to one poor and casual form.
To avoid the deep saves not from storm.
    ' Those things he said, and added more ;
    No clear authenticated lore
I deemed. But now, need now confess
My cultivated narrowness,
Though scarce indeed of sort he meant ?
'Tis the uprooting of content ! '
    So he, the student. 'Twas a mind,
Earnest by nature, long confined
Apart like Vesta in a grove
Collegiate, but let to rove
At last abroad among mankind,
And here in end confronted so
By the true genius, friend or foe,
And actual visage of a place
Before but dreamed of in the glow
Of fancy's spiritual grace.
    Further his meditations aim,
Reverting to his different frame
Bygone. And then : ' Can faith remove
Her light, because of late no plea
I 've lifted to her source above ? '
Dropping thereat upon the knee,
His lips he parted ; but the word
Against the utterance demurred
And failed him. With infirm intent
He sought the house-top. Set of sun :
His feet upon the yet warm stone,
He, Clarel, by the coping leant,
In silent gaze. The mountain town,
A walled and battlemented one,
With houseless suburbs front and rear,
And flanks built up from steeps severe,

Saddles and turrets the ascent—
Tower which rides the elephant.
Hence large the view.   There where he stood,
Was Acra's upper neighbourhood.
The circling hills he saw, with one
Excelling, ample in its crown,
Making the uplifted city low
By contrast—Olivet.   The flow
Of eventide was at full brim ;
Overlooked, the houses sloped from him—
Terraced or domed, unchimnied, gray,
All stone—a moor of roofs.   No play
Of life ; no smoke went up, no sound
Except low hum, and that half drowned.

    The inn abutted on the pool
Named Hezekiah's, a sunken court
Where silence and seclusion rule,
Hemmed round by walls of nature's sort
Base to stone structures seeming one
E'en with the steeps they stand upon.

    As a three-decker's stern-lights peer
Down on the oily wake below,
Upon the sleek dark waters here
The inn's small lattices bestow
A rearward glance.   And here and there
In flaws the languid evening air
Stirs the dull weeds adust, which trail
In festoons from the crag, and veil
The ancient fissures, overtopped
By the tall convent of the Copt,
Built like a light-house o'er the main.

    Blind arches showed in walls of wane,
Sealed windows, portals masoned fast,
And terraces where nothing passed
By parapets all dumb.   No tarn

Among the Kaatskills, high above
Farm-house and stack, last lichened barn
And log-bridge rotting in remove—
More lonesome looks than this dead pool
In town where living creatures rule.

Not here the spell might he undo ;
The strangeness haunted him and grew.

But twilight closes.   He descends
And toward the inner court he wends.

II

ABDON

A LAMP in archway hangs from key—
A lamp whose sidelong rays are shed
On a slim vial set in bed
Of door-post all of masonry.
    That vial hath the Gentile vexed ;
Within it holds Talmudic text,
Or charm. And there the Black Jew sits,
Abdon the host. The lamp-light flits
O'er reverend beard of saffron hue
Sweeping his robe of Indian blue.
    Disturbed and troubled in estate,
Longing for solacement of mate,
Clarel in court there nearer drew,
As yet unnoted, for the host
In meditation seemed engrossed,
Perchance upon some line late scanned
In leathern scroll that drooped from hand.
    Ere long, without surprise expressed,
The lone man marked his lonelier guest,
And welcomed him. Discourse was bred ;
In end a turn it took, and led
To grave recital. Here was one
(If question of his word be none)
Descended from those dubious men,
The unreturning tribes, the Ten
Whom shout and halloo wide have sought,
Lost children in the wood of time.

Yes, he, the Black Jew, stinting naught,
Averred that ancient India's clime
Harboured the remnant of the Tribes,
A people settled with their scribes
In far Cochin.   There was he born
And nurtured, and there yet his kin,
Never from true allegiance torn,
Kept Moses' law.

     Cochin, Cochin
(Mused Clarel), I have heard indeed
Of those Black Jews, their ancient creed
And hoar tradition.   Esdras saith
The Ten Tribes built in Arsareth—
Eastward, still eastward.   That may be.

But look, the scroll of goat-skin, see
Wherein he reads, a wizard book ;
It is the Indian Pentateuch
Whereof they tell.   Whate'er the plea
(And scholars various notions hold
Touching these missing clans of old),
This seems a deeper mystery :
How Judah, Benjamin, live on—
Unmixed into time's swamping sea
So far can urge their Amazon.

He pondered.   But again the host,
Narrating part his life-time tossed,
Told how, long since, with trade in view,
He sailed from India with a Jew
And merchant of the Portuguese
For Lisbon.   More he roved the seas
And marts, till in the last event
He pitched in Amsterdam his tent.

' There had I lived my life,' he said,
' Among my kind, for good they were ;
But loss came—loss, and I was led

To long for Judah—only her.
But see.' He rose, and took the light
And led within : ' There ye espy
What prospect 's left to such as I—
Yonder ! '—a dark slab stood upright
Against the wall ; a rude grave-stone
Sculptured, with Hebrew ciphers strown.
    ' Under Moriah it shall lie—
No distant date, for very soon,
Ere yet a little, and I die.
From Ind to Zion have I come,
But less to live, than end at home.
One other last remove ! ' he sighed,
And meditated on the stone,
Lamp held aloft. That magnified
The hush throughout the dim unknown
Of night—night in a land how dead !
    Thro' Clarel's heart the old man's strain
Dusky meandered in a vein
One with the revery it bred ;
His eyes still dwelling on the Jew
In added dream—so strange his shade
Of swartness like a born Hindoo,
And wizened visage which betrayed
The Hebrew cast. And subtile yet
In ebon frame an amulet
Which on his robe the patriarch wore—
And scroll, and vial in the door,
These too contributed in kind.
    They parted. Clarel sought his cell
Or tomb-like chamber, and—with mind
To break or intermit the spell,
At least perplex it and impede—
Lighted the lamp of olive oil,
And, brushing from a trunk the soil—

'Twas one late purchased at his need—
Opened, and strove to busy him
With small adjustments.   Bootless cheer !
While wavering now, in chanceful skim
His eyes fell on the word JUDÆA
In paper lining of the tray,
For all was trimmed, in cheaper way,
With printed matter.   Curious then
To know this faded denizen,
He read, and found a piece complete,
Briefly comprised in one poor sheet :
          ' The World accosts—
     " Last one out of Holy Land,
What gift bring'st thou ?   Sychem grapes ?
Tabor, which the Eden drapes,
Yieldeth garlands.   I demand
Something cheery at thy hand.
Come, if Solomon's Song thou singest,
Haply Sharon's rose thou bringest."
          ' The Palmer replies :
     " Nay, naught thou nam'st thy servant brings,
Only Judæa my feet did roam ;
And mainly there the pilgrim clings
About the precincts of Christ's tomb.
These palms I bring—from dust not free,
Since dust and ashes both were trod by me." '
     O'er true thy gift (thought Clarel).   Well,
Scarce might the world accept, 'twould seem.
But I, shall *I* my feet impel
Through road like thine and naught redeem ?
Rather thro' brakes, lone brakes, I wind :
As I advance they close behind.—
     Thought's burden : on the couch he throws
Himself and it—rises, and goes
To peer from casement.   'Twas moonlight,

With stars, the Olive Hill in sight,
Distinct, yet dreamy in repose,
As of Katahdin in hot noon,
Lonely, with all his pines in swoon.
   The nature and evangel clashed,
Rather, a double mystery flashed.
Olivet, Olivet do I see ?
The ideal upland, trod by *Thee* ?
   Up or reclined, he felt the soul
Afflicted by that noiseless calm,
Till sleep, the good nurse, deftly stole
The bed beside, and for a charm
Took the pale hand within her own,
Nor left him till the night was gone.

III

In Crete they claimed the tomb of Jove
In glen over which his eagles soar ;
But thro' a peopled town ye rove
To Christ's low urn, where, nigh the door,
Settles the dove.   So much the more
The contrast stamps the human God
Who dwelt among us, made abode
With us, and was of woman born ;
Partook our bread, and thought no scorn
To share the humblest, homeliest hearth,
Shared all of man except the sin and mirth.
Such, among thronging thoughts, may stir
In pilgrim pressing thro' the lane
That dusty wins the reverend fane,
Seat of the Holy Sepulchre,
And naturally named therefrom.
　　　What altars old in cluster rare
And grotto-shrines engird the Tomb :
Caves and a crag ; and more is there ;
And halls monastic join their gloom.
To sum in comprehensive bounds
The Passion's drama with its grounds,
Immense the temple winds and strays
Finding each storied precinct out—
Absorbs the sites all round about—
Omnivorous, and a world of maze.

14

And yet time was when all here stood
Separate, and from rood to rood,
Chapel to shrine, or tent to tent,
Unsheltered still the pilgrim went
Where now enroofed the whole coheres—
Where now thro' influence of years
And spells by many a legend lent,
A sort of nature reappears—
Sombre or sad, and much in tone
Perhaps with that which here was known
Of yore, when from this Salem height,
Then sylvan in primeval plight,
Down came to Shaveh's Dale, with wine
And bread, after the four Kings' check,
The Druid priest Melchizedek,
Abram to bless with rites divine.

What rustlings here from shadowy spaces,
Deep vistas where the votary paces,
Will, strangely intermitting, creep
Like steps in Indian forest deep.
How bird-like steals the singer's note
Down from some rail or arch remote :
While, glimmering where kneelers be,
Small lamps, dispersed, with glow-worm light
Mellow the vast nave's azure night,
And make a haze of mystery :
The blur is spread of thousand years,
And Calvary 's seen as through one's tears.

In cloistral walks the dome detains
Hermits, which during public days
Seclude them where the shadow stays,
But issue when charmed midnight reigns,
Unshod, with tapers lit, and roam,
According as their hearts appoint,
The purlieus of the central Tomb

In round of altars ; and anoint
With fragrant oils each marble shelf :
Or, all alone, strange solace find
And oratory to their mind
Lone locked within the Tomb itself.
    Cells note ye as in bower a nest
Where some sedate rich devotee
Or grave guest-monk from over sea
Takes up through Lent his votive rest,
Adoring from his saintly perch
Golgotha and the guarded Urn,
And mysteries everywhere expressed ;
Until his soul, in rapt sojourn,
Add one more chapel to the Church.
    The friars in turn which tend the Fane,
Dress it and keep, a home make there,
Nor pass for weeks the gate. Again
Each morning they ascend the stair
Of Calvary, with cloth and broom,
For dust thereon will settle down,
And gather, too, upon the Tomb
And places of the Passion's moan.
Tradition, not device and fraud
Here rules—tradition old and broad.
Transfixed in sites the drama 's shown—
Each given spot assigned ; 'tis here
They scourged Him ; soldiers yonder nailed
The Victim to the tree ; in jeer
There stood the Jews ; there Mary paled ;
The vesture was divided here.
    A miracle-play of haunted stone—
A miracle-play, a phantom one,
With power to give pause or subdue.
So that whatever comment be—
Serious, if to faith unknown—

Not possible seems levity
Or aught that may approach thereto.
   And, sooth, to think what numbers here,
Age after age, have worn the stones
In suppliance or judgment fear ;
What mourners—men and women's moans,
Ancestors of ourselves indeed ;
What souls whose penance of remorse
Made poignant by the elder creed,
Found honest language in the force
Of chains entwined that ate the bone ;
How here à Becket's slayers clung
Taking the contrite anguish on,
And, in release from fast and thong,
Buried upon Moriah sleep ;
With more, much more ; such ties, so deep,
Endear the spot, or false or true
As an historic site.   The wrong
Of carpings never may undo
The nerves that clasp about the plea
Tingling with kinship through and through—
Faith childlike and the tried humanity.
   But little here moves hearts of some ;
Rather repugnance grave, or scorn
Or cynicism, to mark the dome
Beset in court or yard forlorn
By pedlars versed in wonted tricks,
Venders of charm or crucifix ;
Or, on saint-days, to hark the din
As during market day at inn,
And polyglot of Asian tongues
And island ones, in interchange
Buzzed out by crowds in costumes strange
Of nations divers.   Are these throngs
Merchants ?   Is this Cairo's bazaar

And concourse ?   Nay, thy strictures bar.
It is but simple nature, see ;
None mean irreverence, though free.
    Unvexed by Europe's grieving doubt
Which asks *And can the Father be ?*
Those children of the climes devout,
On festival in fane installed,
Happily ignorant, make glee
Like orphans in the playground walled.
    Others the duskiness may find
Imbued with more than nature's gloom ;
These, loitering hard by the Tomb,
Alone, and when the day 's declined—
So that the shadow from the stone
Whereon the angel sat is thrown
To distance more, and sigh or sound
Echoes from place of Mary's moan,
Or cavern where the cross was found ;
Or mouse-stir steals upon the ear
From where the soldier reached the spear—
Shrink, much like Ludovico erst
Within the haunted chamber.   Thou,
Less sensitive, yet haply versed
In everything above, below—
In all but thy deep human heart ;
Thyself perchance mayst nervous start
At thine own fancy's final range
Who here wouldst mock : with mystic smart
The subtile Eld can slight avenge.
But gibe—gibe on, until there crawl
About thee in the scorners' seat,
Reactions ; and pride's Smyrna shawl
Plague-strike the wearer.   Ah, retreat !
    But how of some which still deplore
Yet share the doubt ?   Here evermore

'Tis good for such to turn afar
From the Skull's place, even Golgotha,
And view the cedarn dome in sun
Pierced like the marble Pantheon :
No blurring pane, but open sky :
In there day peeps, there stars go by,
And, in still hours which these illume,
Heaven's dews drop tears upon the Tomb.
　　Nor lack there dreams romance can thrill :
In hush when tides and towns are still,
Godfrey and Baldwin from their graves
(Made meetly near the rescued Stone)
Rise, and in arms.　With beaming glaives
They watch and ward the urn they won.
　　So fancy deals, a light achiever :
Imagination, earnest ever,
Recalls the Friday far away,
Relives the crucifixion day—
The Passion and its sequel proves,
Sharing the three pale Marys' frame ;
Thro' the eclipse with these she moves
Back to the house from which they came
To Golgotha.　O empty room,
O leaden heaviness of doom—
O cowering hearts, which sore beset
Deem vain the promise now, and yet
Invoke him who returns no call ;
And fears for more that may befall.
O terror linked with love which cried
' Art gone ? is 't o'er ? and crucified ? '
　　Who might foretell from such dismay
Of blank recoilings, all the blest
Lilies and anthems which attest
The floral Easter holiday ?

IV

OF THE CRUSADERS

WHEN sighting first the towers afar
Which girt the object of the war
And votive march—the Saviour's Tomb,
What made the red-cross knights so shy ?
And wherefore did they doff the plume
And baldrick, kneel in dust, and sigh ?
    Hardly it serves to quote Voltaire
And say they were freebooters—hence,
Incapable of awe or sense
Pathetic ; no, for man is heir
To complex moods ; and in that age
Belief devout and bandit rage
Frequent were joined ; and e'en to-day
At shrines on the Calabrian steep—
Not insincere while feelings sway—
The brigand halts to adore, to weep.
Grant then the worst—is all romance
Which claims that the crusader's glance
Was blurred by tears ?
              But if that round
Of disillusions which accrue
In this our day, imply a ground
For more concern than Tancred knew,
Thinking, yet not as in despair,
Of Christ who suffered for him there
Upon the crag ; then, own it true,

Cause graver much than his is ours
At least to check the hilarious heart
Before these memorable towers.
        But wherefore this ? such theme why start ?
Because if here in many a place
The rhyme—much like the knight indeed—
Abjure brave ornament, 'twill plead
Just reason, and appeal for grace.

V

CLAREL

UPON the morrow's early morn
Clarel is up, and seeks the Urn.
Advancing towards the fane's old arch
Of entrance—curved in sculptured stone,
Dim and defaced, he saw thereon
From rural Bethany the march
Of Christ into another gate—
The golden and triumphal one,
Upon Palm Morn.   For porch to shrine
On such a site, how fortunate
That adaptation of design.
Well might it please.
                    He entered then.
Strangers were there, of each degree,
From Asian shores, with island men,
Mild guests of the Epiphany.

    As when to win the Paschal joy
And Nisan's festal month renew,
The Nazarenes to temple drew,
Even Joseph, Mary, and the BOY,
Whose hand the mother's held ; so here
To later rites and altars dear,
Domestic in devotion's flame
Husbands with wives and children came.

    But he, the student, under dome
Pauses ; he stands before the Tomb.
Through open door he sees the wicks

Alight within, where six and six
For Christ's apostles, night and day,
Lamps, olden lamps do burn.   In smoke
Befogged they shed no vivid ray,
But heat the cell and seem to choke.
   He marked, and revery took flight :
' These burn not like those aspects bright
Of starry watchers when they kept
Vigil at napkined feet and head
Of Him their Lord.—Nay, is He fled ?
Or tranced lies, tranced nor unbewept
With Dorian gods ? or, fresh and clear,
A charm diffused throughout the sphere,
Streams in the ray through yonder dome ?
Not hearsed He is.   But hath ghost home
Dispersed in soil, in sea, in air ?
False Pantheism, false though fair ! '
   So he ; and slack and aimless went,
Nor might untwine the ravelment
Of doubts perplexed.   For easement there
Halting awhile in pillared shade,
A friar he marked, in robe of blue
And round Greek cap of sable hue :
Poor men he led ; much haste he made,
Nor sequence kept, but dragged them so
Hither and thither, to and fro,
To random places.   Might it be
That Clarel, who recoil did here,
Shared but that shock of novelty
Which makes some Protestants unglad
First viewing the mysterious cheer
In Peter's fane ?   Beheld he had,
In Rome beneath the Lateran wall,
The Scala Santa—watched the knees
Of those ascending devotees,

Who, absolution so to reap,
Breathe a low prayer at every step :
    Nay, 'twas no novelty at all.
Nor was it that his nature shrunk
But from the curtness of the monk :
Another influence made swerve
And touched him in profounder nerve.

    He turned, and passing on enthralled,
Won a still chapel ; and one spake
The name.   Brief Scripture, here recalled,
The context less obscure may make :
'Tis writ that in a garden's bound
Our Lord was urned.   On that green ground
He reappeared, by Mary claimed.
The place, or place alleged, is shown—
Arbours congealed to vaults of stone—
The Apparition's chapel named.
This was the spot where now, in frame
Hard to depict, the student came—
The spot where in the dawning gray,
His pallor with night's tears bedewed,
Restored the Second Adam stood—
Not as in Eden stood the First
All ruddy.   Yet, in leaves immersed
And twilight of imperfect day,
Christ seemed the gardener unto her
Misjudging, who in womanhood
Had sought Him late in sepulchre
Embowered, nor found.

                    Here, votive here—
Here by the shrine that Clarel won—
A wreath shed odours.   Scarce that cheer
Warmed some poor Greeks recumbent thrown,
Sore from late journeying far and near,
To hallowed haunts without the town ;

So wearied, that no more they kneeled,
But overnight here laid them down,
Matrons and children, yet unhealed
Of ache. And each face was a book
Of disappointment. ' Why weep'st thou ?
Whom seekest ? '—words, which chanceful now
Recalled by Clarel, he applied
To these before him ; and he took,
In way but little modified,
Part to himself ; then stood in dream
Of all which yet might hap to them.
He saw them spent, provided ill—
Pale, huddled in the pilgrim fleet,
Back voyaging now to homes afar.
Midnight, and rising tempests beat—
Such as St. Paul knew—furious war,
To meet which, slender is the skill.
The lamp that burnt upon the prow
In wonted shrine, extinct is now—
Drowned out with Heaven's last feeble star.
Panic ensues ; their course is turned ;
Toward Tyre they drive—Tyre undiscerned :
A coast of wrecks which warping bleach
On wrecks of piers where eagles screech.

How hopeful from their isles serene
They sailed, and on such tender quest ;
Then, after toils that came between,
They re-embarked ; and, tho' distressed,
Grieved not, for Zion had been seen ;
Each wearing next the heart for charm
Some priestly scrip in leaf of palm.

But these, ah, these in Dawn's pale reign
Asleep upon beach Tyrian !
Or is it sleep ? no, rest—that rest
Which naught shall ruffle or molest.

In gliding turn of dreams which mate
He saw from forth Damascus' gate
Tall Islam in her Mahmal go—
Elected camel, king of all,
In mystic housings draped in flow,
Silk-fringed, with many a silver ball,
Worked ciphers on the Koran's car
And Sultan's cloth.　He hears the jar
Of janizaries armed, a throng
Which drum barbaric, shout and gong
Invest.　And camels—robe and shawl
Of riders which they bear along—
Each sheik a pagod on his tower,
Cross-legged and dusky.　Therewithal,
In affluence of the opal hour,
Curveting troops of Moslem peers
And flash of scimetars and spears
In groves of grass-green pennons fair,
(Like Feiran's palms in fanning air),
Wherefrom the crescent silvery soars.

Then crowds pell-mell, a concourse wild,
Convergings from Levantine shores ;
On foot, on donkeys ; litters rare—
Whole families ; twin panniers piled ;
Rich men and beggars—all beguiled
To cheerful trust in Allah's care ;
Allah, toward whose prophet's urn
And Holy City, fond they turn
As forth in pilgrimage they fare.

But long the way.　And when they note,
Ere yet they pass wide suburbs green,
Some camp in field, nor far remote,
Inviting, pastoral in scene ;
Some child shall leap, and trill in glee
' Mecca, 'tis Mecca, mother—see ! '

Then first she thinks upon the waste
Whither the Simoom maketh haste ;
Where baskets of the white-ribbed dead
Sift the fine sand, while dim ahead
In long, long line, their way to tell,
The bones of camels bleaching dwell,
With skeletons but part interred—
Relics of men which friendless fell ;
Whose own hands, in last office, scooped
Over their limbs the sand, but drooped :
Worse than the desert of the Word,
El Tih, the great, the terrible.
    Ere town and tomb shall greet the eye
Many shall fall, nor few shall die
Which, punctual at set of sun,
Spread the worn prayer-cloth on the sand,
Turning them toward the Mecca stone,
Their shadows ominously thrown
Oblique against the mummy land.
    These pass ; they fade. What next comes near ?
The tawny peasants—human wave
Which rolls over India year by year,
India, the spawning place and grave.
    The turbaned billow floods the plains,
Rolling toward Brahma's rarer fanes—
His Compostel or brown Loret
Where sin absolved, may grief forget.
But numbers, plague-struck, faint and sore,
Drop livid on the flowery shore—
Arrested, with the locusts sleep,
Or pass to muster where no man may peep.
    That vision waned. And, far afloat,
From eras gone he caught the sound
Of hordes from China's furthest moat,
Crossing the Himalayan mound,

To kneel at shrine or relic so
Of Buddha, the Mongolian Fo
Or Indian Saviour.   What profound
Impulsion makes these tribes to range ?
Stable in time's incessant change
Now first he marks, now awed he heeds
The intersympathy of creeds,
Alien or hostile tho' they seem—
Exalted thought or grovelling dream.
    The worn Greek matrons mark him there :
Ah, young, our lassitude dost share ?
Home do thy pilgrim reveries stray ?
Art *thou*, too, weary of the way ?—
    Yes, sympathies of Eve awake ;
Yet do but err.   For how might break
Upon those simple natures true,
The complex passion ? might they view
The apprehension tempest tossed—
The spirit in gulf of dizzying fable lost ?

VI

HE turned to go ; he turned, but stood
In many notes of varying keys,
From shrines like coves in Jordan's wood
Hark to the rival liturgies,
Which, rolling underneath the dome,
Resound about the patient Tomb
And penetrate the aisles. The rite
Of Georgian and Maronite,
Armenian and fervid Greek,
The Latin organ, and wild clash
Of cymbals smitten cheek to cheek
Which the dark Abyssinian sways ;
These like to tides together dash
And question of their purport raise.
     If little of the words he knew,
Might Clarel's fancy forge a clue ?
A malediction seemed each strain—
Himself the mark : O heart profane,
O pilgrim-infidel, begone !
Nor here the sites of Faith pollute,
Thou who misgivest we enthrone
A God untrue, in myth absurd
As monstrous figments blabbed of Jove,
Or, worse, rank lies of Islam's herd :
We know thee, thou there standing mute.
Out, out—begone ! try Nature's reign
Who deem'st the super-nature vain :

To Lot's Wave by black Kedron rove ;
On, by Mount Seir, through Edom move ;
There crouch thee with the jackal down—
Crave solace of the scorpion !
　'Twas fancy, troubled fancy weaved
Those imputations half believed.
The porch he neared ; the chorus swelled ;
He went forth like a thing expelled.
　Yet, going, he could but recall
The wrangles here which oft befall :
Contentions for each holy place,
And jealousies how far from grace :
O, bickering family bereft,
Was feud the heritage He left ?

VII

BEYOND THE WALLS

In street at hand a silence reigns
Which Nature's hush of loneness feigns.
Few casements, few, and latticed deep,
High raised above the head below,
That none might listen, pry, or peep,
Or any hint or inkling know
Of that strange innocence or sin
Which locked itself so close within.
The doors, recessed in massy walls,
And far apart, as dingy were
As Bastille gates.   No shape astir
Except at whiles a shadow falls
Athwart the way, and key in hand
Noiseless applies it, enters so
And vanishes.   By dry airs fanned
The languid hyssop waveth slow,
Dusty, on stones by ruin rent.
'Twould seem indeed the accomplishment
Whereof the greater prophet tells
In truth's forecasting canticles
Where voice of bridegroom, groom and bride
Is hushed.
    Each silent wall and lane—
The city's towers in barren pride
Which still a stifling air detain,
So irked him, with his burden fraught,
Timely the Jaffa Gate he sought,

Thence issued, and at venture went
Along a vague and houseless road
Save narrow houses where abode
The Turk in man's last tenement
Inearthed.   But them he heeded not,
Such trance his reveries begot :
   ' Christ lived a Jew : and in Judæa
May linger any breath of Him ?
If nay, yet surely it is here
One best may learn if all be dim.'
   Sudden it came in random play
' Here to Emmaus is the way ' ;
And Luke's narration straight recurred,
How the two falterers' heart were stirred
Meeting the Arisen (then unknown)
And listening to His lucid word
As here in place they travelled on.
   That scene, in Clarel's temper, bred
A novel sympathy, which said—
I too, I too ; could *I* but meet
Some stranger of a lore replete,
Who, marking how my looks betray
The dumb thoughts clogging here my feet
Would question me, expound and prove,
And make my heart to burn with love—
Emmaus were no dream to-day !
   He lifts his eyes, and, outlined there,
Saw, as in answer to the prayer,
A man who silent came and slow
Just over the intervening brow
Of a nigh slope.   Nearer he drew
Revealed against clear skies of blue ;
And—in that Syrian air of charm—
He seemed, illusion such was given,
Emerging from the level heaven,

And vested with its liquid calm.
  Scarce aged like time's wrinkled sons,
But touched by chastenings of Eld,
Which halloweth life's simpler ones ;
In wasted strength he seemed upheld
Invisibly by faith serene—
Paul's evidence of things not seen.
  No staff he carried ; but one hand
A solitary Book retained.
Meeting the student's, his mild eyes
Fair greeting gave, in faint surprise.
But, noting that untranquil face,
Concern and anxiousness found place
Beyond the occasion and surmise :
   ' Young friend in Christ, what thoughts
    molest
That here ye droop so ? Wanderest
Without a guide where guide should be ?
Receive one, friend : the book—take ye.'
  From man to book in startled way
The youth his eyes bent. Book how gray
And weather-stained in woeful plight—
Much like that scroll left bare to blight,
Which poet pale, when hope was low,
Bade one who into Libya went,
Fling to the wasteful element,
Yes, leave it there, let wither so.
  Ere Clarel ventured on reply
Anew the stranger proffered it,
And in such mode he might espy
It was the page of—Holy Writ.
Then unto him drew Clarel nigher :
' Thou art ? ' ' The sinner Nehemiah.'

VIII

SINNER ?—So spake the saint, a man
Long tarrying in Jewry's court.
With him the faith so well could sort
His home he 'd left, nor turned again,
His home by Narraganset's marge,
Giving those years on death which verge
Fondly to that enthusiast part
Oft coming of a stricken heart
Unselfish, which finds solace so.
   Though none in sooth might hope to know,
And few surmise his forepast bane,
Such needs have been ; since seldom yet
Lone liver was, or wanderer met,
Except he closeted some pain
Or memory thereof.   But thence,
May be, was given him deeper sense
Of all that travail life can lend,
Which man may scarce articulate
Better than herds which share.   What end ?
How hope ? turn whither ? where was gate
For expectation, save the one
Of beryl, pointed by St. John ?
That gate would open, yea, and Christ
Thence issue, come unto His own,
And earth be re-imparadised.
   Passages, presages he knew :
Zion restore, convert the Jew,

34

Reseat him here, the waste bedew ;
Then Christ returneth : so it ran.
  No founded mission chartered him ;
Single in person as in plan,
Absorbed he ranged, in method dim,
A flitting tract-dispensing man :
Tracts in each text scribe ever proved
In East which he of Tarsus roved.
  Though well such heart might sainthood claim,
Unjust alloy to reverence came.
In Smyrna's mart (sojourning there
Waiting a ship for Joppa's stair)
Pestered he passed thro' Gentile throngs
Teased by an eddying urchin host,
His tracts all fluttering like tongues,
The fire-flakes of the Pentecost.
  Deep read he was in seers devout,
The which forecast Christ's second prime,
And on his slate would cipher out
The mystic days and dates sublime,
And ' *Time and times and half a time* '
Expound he could ; and more reveal ;
Yet frequent would he feebly steal
Close to one's side, asking, in way
Of weary age—the hour of day.
But how he lived, and what his fare,
Ravens and angels, few beside,
Dreamed or divined. His garments spare
True marvel seemed, nor unallied
To clothes worn by that wandering band
Which ranged and ranged the desert sand
With Moses ; and for forty years,
Which two-score times reclad the spheres
In green, and plumed the birds anew,
One vesture wore. From home he brought

The garb which still met sun and dew,
Ashen in shade, by rustics wrought.
　　　Latin, Armenian, Greek, and Jew
Full well the harmless vagrant kenned,
The small meek face, the habit gray :
In him they owned our human clay.
The Turk went further : let him wend ;
Him Allah cares for, holy one :
A *Santon* held him ; and was none
Bigot enough scorn's shaft to send.
For, say what cynic will or can,
Man sinless is revered by man
Thro' all the forms which creeds may lend.
　　　And so, secure, nor pointed at,
Among brave Turbans freely roamed the Hat.

IX

' NAY, take it, friend in Christ,' and held
The book in proffer new ; the while
His absent eyes of dreamy Eld
Some floating vision did beguile
(Of heaven perchance the wafted hem),
As if in place of earthly wight
A haze of spirits met his sight,
And Clarel were but one of them.
  ' Consult it, heart ; wayfarer you,
And this a friendly guide, the best ;
No ground there is that faith would view
But here 'tis rendered with the rest ;
The way to fields of Beulah dear
And New Jerusalem is here.'
  ' I know that guide,' said Clarel, ' yes ' ;
And mused awhile in bitterness ;
Then turned and studied him again,
Doubting and marvelling. A strain
Of trouble seamed the elder brow :
' A pilgrim art thou ? pilgrim thou ? '
Words simple, which in Clarel bred
More than the simple saint divined ;
And, thinking of vocation fled,
Himself he asked : or do I rave,
Or have I left now far behind
The student of the sacred lore ?
Direct he then this answer gave :
' I am a traveller—no more.'

'Come then with me, in peace we 'll go ;
These ways of Salem well I know ;
Me let be guide whose guide is this,'
And held the Book in witness so,
As 'twere a guide that could not miss :
'Heart, come with me ; all times I roam,
Yea, everywhere my work I ply,
In Salem's lanes, or down in gloom
Of narrow glens which outer lie :
Ever I find some passer-by.
But thee I 'm sent to ; share and rove,
With me divide the scrip of love.'
    Despite the old man's shattered ray,
Won by his mystic saintly way,
Revering, too, his primal faith,
And grateful for the human claim ;
And deeming he must know each path,
And help him so in languid frame—
The student gave assent, and caught
Dim solacement to previous thought.

X

DAYS fleet.   They rove the storied ground—
Tread many a site that rues the ban
Where serial wrecks on wrecks confound
Era and monument and man ;
Or rather, in stratifying way
Bed and impact and overlay.
The Hospitallers' cloisters shamed
Crumble in ruin unreclaimed
On shivered Fatamite palaces
Reared upon crash of Herod's sway—
In turn built on the Maccabees,
And on King David's glory, they ;
And David on antiquities
Of Jebusites and Ornan's floor,
And hunters' camps of ages long before.
So Glenroy's tiers of beaches be—
Abandoned margins of the Glacial Sea.
        Amid that waste from joy debarred,
How few the islets fresh and green ;
Yet on Moriah, tree and sward
In Allah's courts park-like were seen
From roof near by ; below, fierce ward
Being kept by Mauritanian guard
Of bigot blacks.   But of the reign
Of Christ did no memento live
Save soil and ruin ?   Negative
Seemed yielded in that crumbling fane,

Erst gem to Baldwin's sacred fief,
The chapel of our Dame of Grief.
    But hard by Ophel's winding base,
Well watered by the runnel led,
A spot they found, not lacking grace,
Named Garden of King Solomon,
Tho' now a cauliflower-bed
To serve the kitchens of the town.
    One day as here they came from far,
The saint repeated with low breath,
' Adonijah, Adonijah—
The stumbling-stone of Zoheleth.'
He wanders, Clarel thought—but no,
For text and chapter did he show
Narrating how the prince in glade,
This very one, the banquet made,
The plotters' banquet, long ago,
Even by the stone named Zoheleth ;
But startled by the trump that blew,
Proclaiming Solomon, pale grew
With all his guests.
                From lower glen
They slanted up the steep, and there
Attained a higher terraced den,
Or small and silent field, quite bare.
The mentor breathed : ' Come early here
A sign thou 'lt see.'—Clarel drew near ;
' What sign ? ' he asked.   Whereto with sighs :
' Abashed by morning's holy eyes
This field will crimson, and for shame.'
    Struck by his fantasy and frame,
Clarel regarded him for time,
Then noted that dull reddish soil,
And caught sight of a thing of grime
Whose aspect made him to recoil—

A rotting charnel-house forlorn
Midway inearthed, caved in and torn.
And Clarel knew—one scarce might err—
The field of blood, the bad Aceldama.

By Olivet in waning day
The saint in fond illusion went,
Dream mixed with legend and event ;
And as with reminiscence fraught,
Narrated in his rambling way
How here at eve was Christ's resort,
The last low sheep-bell tinkling lone—
Christ and the dear disciple—John.

Oft by the Golden Gate that looks
On Shaveh down, and far across
Toward Bethany's secluded nooks—
That gate which sculptures rare emboss
In arches twin ; the same where rode
Christ entering with secret load—
Same gate, or on or near the site—
When palms were spread to left and right
Before Him, and with sweet acclaim
Were waved by damsels under sway
Of trees wherefrom those branches came—
Over and under palms He went
Unto that crown how different !
The port walled up by Moslem hands
In dread of that predicted day
When pealing hymns, armed Christian bands—
So Islam seers despondent vouch—
Shall storm it, wreathed in Mary's May :
By that sealed gate, in languor's slouch,
How listless in the golden day,
Clarel the mentor frequent heard
The time for Christ's return allot :
A dream, and like a dream it blurred

The sense—faded, and was forgot.
Moved by some mystic impulse, far
From motive known or regular,
The saint would thus his lore unfold,
Though inconclusive ; yes, half told
The theme he 'd leave, then nod, droop, doze—
Start up and prattle—sigh, and close.

XI

LOWER GIHON

WELL for the student, might it last,
This dreamful frame which Lethe bred :
Events obtruded, and it passed.
For on a time the twain were led
From Gihon's upper pool and glade
Down to the deeper gulf. They strayed
Along by many silent cells
Cut in the rock, void citadels
Of death. In porch of one was seen
A mat of tender turf, faint green ;
And quiet standing on that sward
A stranger whom they overheard
Low murmuring—' Equivocal !
Woo'st thou the weary to thee—tell,
Thou tomb, so winsome in thy grace ?
To me no reassuring place.'
　　He saw them not ; and they, to shun
Disturbing him, passed, and anon
Met three demoniacs, sad three
Ranging those wasteful limits o'er
As in old time. That look they wore
Which in the moody mad bids flee :
'Tis—What have I to do with thee ?
　　Two shunned approach. But one did sit
Lost in some reminiscence sore
Of private wrong outrageous. He,
As at the larger orb of it,

Looming through mists of mind, would bound,
Or cease to pore upon the ground
As late ; and so be inly riven
By arrows of indignant pain :
Convulsed in face, he glared at heaven
Then lapsed in sullenness again.
  Dire thoughts the pilgrim's mind beset :
' And did Christ come ? in such a scene
Encounter the poor Gadarene
Long centuries ago ? and yet—
Behold ! '
    But here came in review—
Though of their nearness unaware—
The stranger, downward wending there,
Who, marking Clarel, instant knew—
At least so might his start declare—
A brother that he well might own
In tie of spirit.   Young he was,
With crescent forehead—but alas,
Of frame misshaped.   Word spake he none,
But vaguely hovered, as may one
Not first who would accost, but deep
Under reserve the wish may keep.
Ere Clarel, here embarrassed grown,
Made recognition, the Unknown
Compressed his lips, turned, and was gone.
Mutely for moment, face met face :
But more perchance between the two
Was interchanged than e'en may pass
In many a worded interview.
  The student in his heart confessed
A novel sympathy impressed ;
And late remissness to retrieve
Fain the encounter would renew.
And yet—if oft one's resolution

Be overruled by constitution—
Herein his heart he might deceive.
   Ere long, retracing higher road,
Clarel with Nehemiah stood
By David's Tower, without the wall,
Where black the embattled shadows fall
At morn over Hinnom. Groups were there
Come out to take the evening air,
Watching a young lord Turk in pride,
With fez and sash as red as coral,
And on a steed whose well-groomed hide
Was all one burnished burning sorrel,
Scale the lit slope ; then veering wide,
Rush down into the gloomful gorge,
The steel hoof showering sparks as from a forge.
Even Nehemiah, in senile tone
Of dreamy interest, was won
That shooting star to gaze upon.
   But rallying, he bent his glance
Toward the opposing eminence ;
And turning, ' Seest thou not,' he said,
' As sinks the sun beyond this glen
Of Moloch, how clouds intervene
And hood the brightness that was shed ?
But yet few hours and he will rise
In better place, and beauty get ;
Yea, friend in Christ, in morning skies
Return he will over Olivet :
And we shall greet him. Say ye so ?
Betimes then will we up and go.
Farewell. At early dawn await
Christ's bondman old at Stephen's Gate.'

XII

CELIO

BUT ere they meet in place assigned,
It needs—to make the sequel clear—
A crossing thread be first entwined.
    Within the Terra-Santa's wall
(A prefix dropped, the Latins here
So the Franciscan Convent call),
Commended to the warden's care,
The mitred father-warden there,
By missives from a cardinal,
It chanced an uncompanioned youth,
By birth a Roman, shelter found.
In casual contact, daily round,
Mixed interest the stranger won.
Each friar, the humblest, could but own
His punctual courtesy, in sooth,
Though this still guarded a reserve
Which, not offending, part estranged.
Sites, sites and places all he ranged
Unwearied, but would ever swerve
From escort such as here finds place,
Or cord-girt guide, or chamberlain
Martial in Oriental town,
By gilt-globed staff of office known,
Sword by his side, in golden lace,
Tall herald making clear the van.
    But what most irked each tonsured man,

Distrust begat, concern of heart
Was this : though the young man took part
In chapel service, 'twas as guest
Who but conformed ; he showed no zest
Of faith within, faith personal.
Ere long the warden, kindly all,
Said inly with himself : Poor boy,
Enough hast thou of life-annoy ;
Let be reproach.   Tied up in knot
Of body by the fleshly withes,
Needs must it be the spirit writhes
And takes a warp.   But Christ will blot
Some records in the end.
                       And own,
So far as *in* by *out* is shown,
Not idle was the monk's conceit.
Fair head was set on crook and lump,
Absalom's locks but Æsop's hump,
Deep in the grave eyes' last retreat,
One read thro' guarding feint of pride,
Quick sense of all the ills that gride
In one contorted so.   But here,
More to disclose in bearing chief,
More than to monks might well appear,
There needs some running mention brief.

   Fain had his brethren have him grace
Some civic honorable place ;
And interest was theirs to win
Ample preferment ; he as kin
Was loved, if but ill understood :
At heart they had his worldly good ;
But he postponed, and went his way
Unpledged, unhampered.   So that still
Leading a studious life at will,
And prompted by an earnest mind,

Scarce might he shun the fevered sway
Of focused question in our day.
Overmuch he shared, but in that kind
Which marks the Italian turn of thought,
When, counting Rome's tradition naught,
The mind is coy to own the rule
Of sect replacing, sect or school.
At sea, in brig which swings no boat,
To founder is to sink.

                     On day
When from St. Peter's balcony,
The raised pontific fingers bless
The city and the world ; the stress
He knew of fate : Blessest thou *me*,
One wave here in this heaving sea
Of heads ? how may a blessing be ?
Luckless, from action's thrill removed,
And all that yields our nature room ;
In courts a jest ; and, harder doom,
Never the hunchback may be loved.
Never ! for Beatrice—*Bice*—O,
Diminutive once sweet, made now
All otherwise !—didst thou but fool ?
Arch practice in precocious school ?
Nay, rather 'twas ere thou didst bud
Into thy riper womanhood.

      Since love, arms, courts, abjure—why then
Remaineth to me what ? the pen ?
Dead feather of ethereal life !
Nor efficacious much, save when
It makes some fallacy more rife.
My kin—I blame them not at heart—
Would have me act some routine part,
Subserving family, and dreams
Alien to me—illusive schemes.

This world clean fails me : still I yearn.
Me then it surely does concern
Some other world to find. But where ?
In creed ? I do not find it there.
That said, and is the emprise o'er ?
Negation, is there nothing more ?
This side the dark and hollow bound
Lies there no unexplored rich ground ?
Some other world : well, there 's the *New*—
Ah, joyless and ironic too !
    They vouch that virgin sphere 's assigned
Seat for man's re-created kind :
Last hope and proffer, they protest.
Brave things ! sun rising in the west ;
And bearded centuries but gone
For ushers to the beardless one.
Nay, nay ; your future 's too sublime :
The Past, the Past is half of time,
The proven half.—Thou Pantheon old
Two thousand years have round thee rolled ;
Yet thou, in Rome, thou bid'st me seek
Wisdom in something more antique
Than thou thyself. Turn then : what seer,
The senior of this Latian one,
Speaks from the ground, transported here
In Eastern soil ? Far buried down—
For consecration and a grace
Enlocking Santa Croce's base—
Lies earth of Jewry, which of yore
The homeward bound Crusaders bore
In fleet from Jaffa.—Trajan's hall,
That huge ellipse imperial,
Was built by Jews. And Titus' Arch
Transmits their conqueror in march
Of trophies which those piers adorn.

D

There yet, for an historic plea,
In heathen triumph's harlotry
The Seven-Branched Candlestick is borne.
    What then ?   Tho' all be whim of mine,
Yet by these monuments I 'm schooled,
Arrested, strangely overruled ;
Methinks I catch a beckoning sign,
A summons as from Palestine.
Yea, let me view that pontiff-land
Whose sway occult can so command ;
Make even Papal Rome to be
Her appanage or colony.
Is Judah's mummy quite unrolled ?
To pluck the talisman from fold !
    But who may well indeed forecast
The novel influence of scenes
Remote from his habitual Past
The unexpected supervenes ;
Which Celio proved.   'Neath Zion's lee
His nature, with that nature blent,
Evoked an upstart element,
As do the acid and the alkali.

XIII

THE ARCH

BLUE-LIGHTS sent up by ship forlorn
Are answered oft but by the glare
Of rockets from another, torn
In the same gale's inclusive snare.

    'Twas then when Celio was lanced
By novel doubt, the encounter chanced
In Gihon, as recited late,
And at a time when Clarel too,
On his part, felt the grievous weight
Of those demoniacs in view ;
So that when Celio advanced
No wonder that the meeting eyes
Betrayed reciprocal surmise
And interest.   'Twas thereupon
The Italian, as the eve drew on,
Regained the gate, and hurried in
As he would passionately win
Surcease to thought by rapid pace.
Eastward he bent, across the town,
Till in the Via Crucis lone
An object there arrested him.
    With gallery which years deface,
Its bulk athwart the alley grim,
The arch named Ecce Homo threw ;
The same, if childlike faith be true,
From which the Lamb of God was shown
By Pilate to the wolfish crew.

And Celio—in frame how prone
To kindle at that scene recalled—
Perturbed he stood, and heart-enthralled.
    No raptures which with saints prevail,
Nor trouble of compunction born
He felt, as there he seemed to scan
Aloft in spectral guise, the pale
Still face, the purple robe, and thorn ;
And inly cried—*Behold the Man !*
Yon Man it is this burden lays :
Even He who in the pastoral hours,
Abroad in fields, and cheered by flowers,
Announced a heaven's unclouded days ;
And, ah, with such persuasive lips—
Those lips now sealed while doom delays—
Won men to look for solace there ;
But, crying out in death's eclipse,
When rainbow none His eyes might see,
Enlarged the margin for despair—
My God, My God, forsakest Me ?
    Upbraider ! we upbraid again ;
Thee we upbraid ; our pangs constrain
Pathos itself to cruelty.
Ere yet Thy day no pledge was given
Of homes and mansions in the heaven—
Paternal homes reserved for us ;
Heart hoped it not, but lived content—
Content with life's own discontent,
Nor deemed that fate ere swerved for us :
The natural law men let prevail ;
Then reason disallowed the state
Of instinct's variance with fate.
But Thou—ah, see, in rack how pale
Who did the world with throes convulse ;
Behold Him—yea—behold the Man

Who warranted if not began
The dream that drags out its repulse.
    Nor less some cannot break from Thee ;
Thy love so locked is with Thy lore,
They may not rend them and go free :
The head rejects ; so much the more
The heart embraces—what ? the love ?
If true what priests avouch of Thee,
The shark Thou mad'st, yet claim'st the dove.
    Nature and Thee in vain we search :
Well urged the Jews within the porch—
' How long wilt make us still to doubt ? '
How long ?—'Tis eighteen cycles now—
Enigma and evasion grow ;
And shall we never find Thee out ?
What isolation lones Thy state
That all we else know cannot mate
With what Thou teachest ?   Nearing Thee
All footing fails us ; history
Shows there a gulf where bridge is none !
In lapse of unrecorded time,
Just after the apostles' prime,
What chance or craft might break it down ?
Served this a purpose ?   By what art
Of conjuration might the heart
Of heavenly love, so sweet, so good,
Corrupt into the creeds malign,
Begetting strife's pernicious brood,
Which claimed for patron Thee divine ?
    Anew, anew,
For this Thou bleedest, Anguished Face ;
Yea, Thou through ages to accrue,
Shalt the Medusa shield replace :
In beauty and in terror too
Shalt paralyse the nobler race—

Smite or suspend, perplex, deter—
Tortured, shalt prove a torturer.
Whatever ribald Future be,
Thee shall these heed, amaze their hearts with
    Thee—
Thy white, Thy red, Thy fairness and Thy tragedy.

He turned, uptorn in inmost frame,
Nor weened he went the way he came,
Till meeting two there, nor in calm—
A monk and layman, one in creed,
The last with novice-ardour warm,
Newcomer, and devout indeed,
To whom the other was the guide,
And showed the Places. 'Here,' he cried,
At pause before a wayside stone,
'Thou mark'st the spot where that bad Jew
His churlish taunt at Jesus threw
Bowed under cross with stifled moan :
Caitiff, which for that cruel wrong
Thenceforth till Doomsday drives along.'
Starting, as here he made review,
Celio winced—Am *I* the Jew ?
Without delay, afresh he turns
Descending by the Way of Thorns,
Winning the Proto-Martyr's gate,
And goes out down Jehoshaphat.
Beside him slid the shadows flung
By evening from the tombstones tall
Upon the bank far sloping from the wall.
Scarce did he heed, or did but slight
The admonishment the warder rung
That with the setting of the sun,
Now getting low and all but run,
The gate would close, and for the night.

XIV

IF Savonarola's zeal devout
But with the faggot's flame died out ;
If Leopardi, stoned by Grief,
A young St. Stephen of the Doubt,
Might merit well the martyr's leaf ;
In these if passion held her claim,
Let Celio pass, of breed the same,
Nor ask from him—not found in them—
The Attic calm or Saxon phlegm.

    Night glooming now in valley dead,
The Italian turned, regained the gate,
But found it closed, the warder fled,
And strange hush of an Eastern town
Where life retreats with set of sun.
Before the riveted clamped wood
Alone in outer dark he stood.
A symbol is it ? be it so :
Harbour remains, I 'll thither go.

    A point there is where Kedron's shore,
Narrowing, deepening, steepening more,
Shrinks to an adamantine pass
Flanked by three tombs, from base to head
Hewn from the cliff in cubic mass,
One quite cut off and islanded,
And one presents in Petra row
Pillars in hanging portico

55

Or balcony, here looking down
Vacantly on the vacant glen :
A place how dead, hard by a town.
'Twas here that Celio made his den
Where erst, as by tradition held,
St. James from hunters lay concealed,
Levites and bigots of the thong.

    Hour after hour slow dragged along.
The glen's wall with night round about
Blended as cloud with cloud-rack may.
But lo—as when off Tamura
The splash of north-lights on the sea
Crimsons the bergs—so here start out
Some crags aloft how vividly.

    Apace he won less narrow bound.
From the high gate, behold, a stream
Of torches.   Lava-like it wound
Out from the city locked in dream,
And red adown the valley flowed.
Was it his friends the friars ? from height
Meet rescue bringing in that light
To one benighted ?   Yes, they showed
A file of monks.   But—how ? their wicks
Invest a shrouded crucifix ;
And each with flambeau held in hand,
Craped laymen mingle with the band
Of cord-girt gowns.   He looks again :
Yes, 'tis the Terra Santa's train.
Nearer they come.   The warden goes,
And other faces Celio knows.
Upon an office these are bound
Consolatory, which may stem
The affliction or relieve the wound
Of those which mute accompany them
In mourners' garb.

Aside he shrunk
Until had passed the rearmost monk ;
Then, cloaked, he followed them in glade
Where fell the shadow deeper made.
Kedron they cross.   Much so might move—
If legend hold, which none may prove—
The remnant of the Twelve which bore
Down thro' this glen in funeral plight
The Mother of our Lord by night
To sepulchre.   Nay, just before
Her tomb alleged, the monks and they
Which mourn pause and uplift a lay ;
Then rise, pass on, and bow the knee
In dust beside Gethsemane.

One named the Bitter Cup, and said :
' Saviour, Thou knowest : it was here
The angels ministered, Thy head
Supported, kissed Thy lidded eyes
And pale swooned cheek till Thou didst rise ;
Help these then, unto these come near ! '

Out sobbed the mourners, and the tear
From Celio trickled ; but he mused—
Weak am I, by a myth abused.

Up Olivet the torchlight train
Filed slowly, yielding tribute-strain
At every sacred place they won ;
Nor tarried long, but journeyed on
To Bethany—thro' stony lane
Went down into the narrow house
Or void cave named from Lazarus.
The flambeaux redden the dark wall,
Their shadows on that redness fall.
To make the attestation rife,
The resurrection and the life
Through Him the lord of miracle—

The warden from the page doth bruit
The story of the man that died
And lived again—bound hand and foot
With grave-clothes, rose—electrified ;
Whom then they loosed, let go ; even he
Whom many people came to see,
The village hinds and farm-house maids,
Afterward, at the supper given
To Jesus in the balmy even,
Who raised him vital from the shades.
The lesson over, well they sang
' *O death, where is thy sting ?   O grave,*
Where is thy victory ? ' It rang,
And ceased.   And from the outward cave
These tones were heard : ' But died he twice ?
He comes not back from Paradise
Or Hades now.   A vacant tomb
By Golgotha they show—a cell,
A void cell here.   And is it well ?
Raiser and raised divide one doom ;
Both vanished now.'
　　　　　　　　　　　No thrills forewarn
Of fish that leaps from midnight tarn ;
The very wave from which it springs
Is startled and recoils in rings.
So here with Celio and the word
Which from his own rash lips he heard.
He, hastening forth now all unseen,
Recrossed the mountain and ravine,
Nor paused till on a mound he sate
Biding St. Stephen's opening gate.
　　　Ere long in gently fanning flaws
An odoriferous balmy air
Foreruns the morning, then withdraws,
Or—westward heralding—roves there.

The startled East a tremor knows—
Flushes—anon superb appears
In state of housings, shawls and spears,
Such as the Sultan's vanguard shows.
    Preceded thus, in pomp the sun
August from Persia draweth on,
Waited by groups upon the wall
Of Judah's upland capital.

XV

UNDER THE MINARET

Lo, shoot the spikes above the hill :
Now expectation grows and grows ;
Yet vain the pageant, idle still :
When one would get at Nature's will—
To be put off by purfled shows !
  He breaks. Behold, thou orb supreme,
'Tis Olivet which thou ascendest—
The hill and legendary chapel ;
Yet how indifferent thy beam !
Awe nor reverence pretendest :
Dome and summit dost but dapple
With gliding touch, a tinging gleam :
Knowest thou the Christ ? believest in the
   dream ?
   'Twas Celio—seated there, as late,
Upon the mound. But now the gate
Flung open, welcomes in the day,
And lets out Clarel with the guide ;
These from the wall had hailed the ray ;
And Celio heard them there aside,
And turning, rose. Was it to greet ?
  But ere they might accost or meet,
From minaret in grounds hard by
Of Omar, the muezzin's cry—
Tardy, for Mustapha was old,
And age a laggard is—was rolled,

Announcing Islam's early hour
Of orison.   Along the walls
And that deep gulf over which these tower—
Far down toward Rogel, hark, it calls !
Can Siloa hear it, yet her wave
So listless lap the hollow cave ?
Is Zion deaf ?   But, promptly still,
Each turban at that summons shrill,
Which should have called ere perfect light,
Bowed—hands on chest, or arms upright ;
While over all those fields of loss
Where now the Crescent rides the Cross,
Sole at the marble mast-head stands
The Islam herald, his two hands
Upon the rail, and sightless eyes
Turned upward reverent toward the skies.
And none who share not this defect
The rules to function here elect ;
Since, raised upon the lifted perch
What leave for prying eyes to search
Into the privacies that lurk
In courts domestic of the Turk,
Whose tenements in every town
Guard well against the street alone.
      But what 's evoked in Clarel's mien—
What look, responsive look is seen
In Celio, as together there
They pause ?   Can these a climax share ?
Mutual in approach may glide
Minds which from poles adverse have come,
Belief and unbelief ? may doom
Of doubt make such to coincide—
Upon one frontier brought to dwell
Arrested by the Ezan high
In summons as from out the sky

To matins of the infidel ?
The God alleged, here in abode
Ignored with such impunity,
Scarce true is writ a jealous God.
        Think ye such thoughts ?   If so it be,
Yet these may eyes transmit and give ?
Mere eyes ? so quick, so sensitive ?
        Howbeit Celio knew his mate :
Again, as down in Gihon late,
He hovered with his overture—
An overture that scorned debate.
But inexperienced, shy, unsure—
Challenged abrupt, or yea or nay,
Again did Clarel hesitate ;
When quick the proud one with a look
Which might recoil of heart betray,
And which the other scarce might brook
In recollection, turned away.
        Ah, student, ill thy sort have sped :
The instant proffer—it is fled !
        When, some days after, for redress
Repentant Clarel sought access,
He learned the name, with this alone—
From convent Celio was gone,
Nor knew they whither.
                        Here in press
To Clarel came a dreamy token :
What speck is that so far away
That wanes and wanes in waxing day ?
Is it the sail ye fain had spoken
Last night when surges parted ye ?
But on, it is a boundless sea.

XVI

THE WALL OF WAIL

BENEATH the toppled ruins old
In series from Moriah rolled
Slips Kedron furtive ? underground,
Peasants avouch they hear the sound.
In aisled lagunes and watery halls
Under the temple, silent sleep
What memories elder ? Far and deep
What ducts and chambered wells and walls.
And many deep substructions be
Which so with doubt and gloom agree,
To question one is borne along—
Based these the Right ? subserved the Wrong ?
 'Twas by an all-forgotten way,
Whose mouth in outer glen forbid
By heaps of rubbish long lay hid,
Cloaca of remotest day ;
'Twas by that unsuspected vault
With outlet in mid city lone,
A spot with ruin all bestrown—
The peasants in sedition late
Captured Jerusalem in strait,
Took it by underground assault.
 Go wander, and within the walls,
Among the glades of cactus trees
Where no life harbours, peers or calls—
Wild solitudes like shoals in seas
Unsailed ; or list at still sundown,
List to the hand-mills as they drone,

Domestic hand-mills in the court,
And groups there in the dear resort,
Mild matron pensive by her son,
The little prattler at her knee :
Under such scenes abysses be—
Dark quarries where few care to pry,
Whence came those many cities high—
Great capitals successive reared,
And which successive disappeared
On this same site.   To powder ground,
Dispersed their dust blows round and round.
　　　No shallow gloss may much avail
When these or kindred thoughts assail :
Which Clarel proved, the more he went
A rover in their element.
For—trusting still that in some place
Where pilgrims linger he anew
The missing stranger yet would face
And speak with—never he withdrew
His wandering feet.
　　　　　　　　In aimless sort
Passing across the town amort,
They came where camped in corner waste,
Some Edomites were at repast—
Sojourners mere, and of a day—
Dark-hued, nor unlike birds of prey
Which on the stones of Tyre alight.
While Clarel fed upon that sight—
The saint repeating in his ear
Meet text applying to the scene—
As liberated from ravine,
Voices in choral note they hear ;
And, strange as lilies in morass,
At the same moment, lo, appear
Emerging from a stony pass,

A lane low-vaulted and unclean,
Damsels in linen robes, heads bare,
Enlinked with matrons pacing there,
And elders gray ; the maids with book :
Companions would one page o'erlook ;
And vocal thus they wound along,
No glad procession, spite the song.
For truth to own, so downcast they—
At least the men, in sordid dress
And double file—the slim array,
But for the maidens' gentleness
And voices which so bird-like sang,
Had seemed much like a coffle gang.
    But Nehemiah a key supplied :
' Alas, poor misled Jews,' he sighed,
' Ye do but dirge among your dead.—
The Hebrew quarter here we tread ;
And this is Friday ; Wailing Day :
These to the Temple wend their way.
And shall we follow ? ' Doing so
They came upon a sunken yard
Obscure, where dust and rubbish blow.
Felonious place, and quite debarred
From common travel. On one side
A blind wall rose, stable and great—
Massed up immense, an Ararat
Founded on bevelled blocks how wide,
Reputed each a stone august
Of Solomon's fane (else fallen to dust)
But now adopted for the wall
To Islam's courts. There, lord of all,
The Turk permits the tribes to creep
Abject in rear of those dumb stones,
To lean or kneel, lament and weep ;
Sad mendicants shut out from gate

Inexorable.   Sighs and groans :
To be restored ! we wait, long wait !
They call to count their pristine state
On this same ground : the lifted rows
Of peristyles ; the porticoes
Crown upon crown, where Levite trains
In chimes of many a silver bell
(Daintily small as pearls in chain)
Hemming their mantles musical—
Passed in procession up and down,
Viewing the belt of guarding heights,
And march of shadows there, and flights
Of pigeon-pets, and palm leaves blown ;
Or heard the silver trumpets call—
The priestly trumps, to festival.
So happy they ; such Judah's prime.
But we, the remnant, lo, we pale ;
Cast from the Temple, here we wail—
Yea, perish ere come Shiloh's time.

    Hard by that joyless crew which leant
With brows against the adamant—
Sad buttresses thereto—hard by—
The student marks the Black Jew bowed :
His voice he hears amid the crowd
Which supplicate stern Shaddei.
And earnest, too, he seeth there
One scarcely Hebrew in his dress
Rural, and hard cheek's swarthiness,
With nothing of an Eastern air.
His eyes met Clarel's unremoved—
In end a countryman he proved,
A strange apostate.   On the twain
Contrasted so—the white, the black—
Man's earliest breed and latest strain—
Behind the master Moslem's back
Skulking, and in great Moses' track—

Gazed Clarel with the wonderment
Of wight who feels the earth upheave
Beneath him, and learns, ill-content
That terra firma can deceive.

    When now those Friday wails were done,
Nehemiah, sidling with his book
Unto a lorn decrepit one,
Proffered a tract : ' 'Tis Hebrew, look,'
Zealous he urged ; ' it points the way,
.Sole way, dear heart, whereby ye may
Rebuild the Temple.'   Answer none
Gat he from Isaac's pauper son,
Who, turning, part as in disdain,
Crept toward his squalid home.   Again
Enrapt stood Clarel, lost awhile :
' Yon Jew has faith ; can faith be vain ?
But *is* it faith ? ay, faith 's the word—
What else ?   Faith then can thus beguile
Her faithfulest.   Hard, that is hard ! '
So doubts invaded, found him out.
He strove with them ; but they proved stout,
Nor would they down.

                But turn regard.
Among the maids those rites detained,
One he perceived, as it befell,
Whose air expressed such truth unfeigned,
And harmonies inlinked which dwell
In pledges born of record pure—
She looked a legate to insure
That Paradise is possible
Now as hereafter.   'Twas the grace
Of Nature's dawn : an Eve-like face
And Nereid eyes with virgin spell
Candid as day, yet baffling quite
Like day, through unreserve of light.
A dove, she seemed, a temple dove,

Born in the temple or its grove,
And nurtured there.   But deeper viewed,
What was it that looked part amiss ?
A bit impaired ? what lack of peace ?
Enforced suppression of a mood,
Regret with yearning intertwined,
And secret protest of a virgin mind.

Hebrew the profile, every line ;
But as in haven fringed with palm,
Which Indian reefs embay from harm,
Belulled as in the vase the wine—
Red-budded corals in remove,
Peep coy through quietudes above ;
So through clear olive of the skin,
And features finely Hagarene ;
Its way a tell-tale flush did win—
A tint which unto Israel's sand
Blabbed of the June in some far clover land.

Anon by chance the damsel's eye
Fell on Nehemiah, and the look
A friendly recognition spoke,
Returned in kind.   When by and by
The groups brake up and homeward bent ;
Then, nor unnoted by the youth,
That maiden with the apostate went,
Whose voice paternal called her—' Ruth ! '

' Tell, friend,' said Clarel eagerly,
As from the wall of wail they passed ;
' Father and daughter ?   Who may be
That strange pervert ? '   No willing haste
The mentor showed ; a while he fed
On anxious thoughts ; then grievingly
The story gave—a tangled thread,
Which, cleared from snarl and ordered so,
Follows transferred, with interflow
Of much Nehemiah scarce might add.

XVII

NATHAN

NATHAN had sprung from worthy stock—
Austere, ascetical, but free,
Which hewed their way from sea-beat rock
Wherever woods and winter be.
      The pilgrim-keel in storm and stress
Had erred, and on a wilderness.
But shall the children all be schooled
By hap which their forefathers ruled ?
Those primal settlers put in train
New emigrants which inland bore ;
From these, too, emigrants again
Westward pressed further ; more bred more ;
At each remove a goodlier wain,
A heart more large, an ampler shore,
With legacies of farms behind ;
Until in years the wagons wind
Through parks and pastures of the sun,
Warm plains as of Esdraelon :
'Tis nature in her best benign.
Wild, wild in symmetry of mould,
With freckles on her tawny gold,
The lily alone looks pantherine—
The libbard-lily.   Never broods
The gloom here of grim hemlock woods
Breeding the witchcraft-spell malign ;
But groves like isles in Grecian seas,
Those dotting isles, the Sporades.

But who the gracious charm may tell—
Long rollings of the vast serene—
The prairie in her swimming swell
Of undulation.
             Such glad scene
Was won by venturers from far
Born under that severer star
The landing patriarchs knew. In fine,
To Illinois—a turf divine
Of promise, how auspicious spread,
Ere yet the cities rose thereon—
From Saco's mountain wilds were led
The sire of Nathan, wife and son ;
Life's lot to temper so, and shun
Mountains whose camp withdrawn was set
Above one vale he would forget.
    After some years their tale had told,
He rested ; lay forever stilled
With sachems and mound-builders old.
The son was grown ; the farm he tilled ;
A stripling, but of manful ways,
Hardy and frugal, oft he filled
The widow's eyes with tears of praise.
An only child, with her he kept
For *her* sake part, the Christian way,
Though frequent in his bosom crept
Precocious doubt unbid. The sway
He felt of his grave life, and power
Of vast space, from the log-house door
Daily beheld. Three Indian mounds
Against the horizon's level bounds
Dim showed across the prairie green
Like dwarfed and blunted mimic shapes
Of Pyramids at distance seen
From the broad Delta's planted capes

Of vernal grain. In nearer view
With trees he saw them crowned, which
    drew
From the red sagamores of eld
Entombed within, the vital gum
Which green kept each mausoleum.

    Hard by, as chanced, he once beheld
Bones like sea corals ; one bleached skull
A vase vined round and beautiful
With flowers ; felt, with bated breath
The floral revelry over death.

    And other sights his heart had thrilled ;
Lambs had he known by thunder killed,
Innocents—and the type of Christ
Betrayed. Had not such things sufficed
To touch the young pure heart with awe,
Memory's mint could move him more.
In prairie twilight, summer's own,
The last cow milked, and he alone
In barn-yard dreamy by the fence,
Contrasted, came a scene immense :
The great White Hills, mount flanked by
    mount,
The Saco and Ammonoosuc's fount ;
Where, in September's equinox
Nature hath put such terror on
That from his mother man would run—
Our mother, Earth : the founded rocks
Unstable prove : the Slide ! the Slide !
Again he saw the mountain side
Sliced open ; yet again he stood
Under its shadow, on the spot—
Now waste, but once a cultured plot,
Though far from village neighbourhood—
Where, nor by sexton hearsed at even,

Somewhere his uncle slept ; no mound,
Since not a trace of him was found,
So whelmed the havoc from the heaven.
    This reminiscence of dismay,
These thoughts unhinged him.   On a day
Waiting for monthly grist at mill
In settlement some miles away,
It chanced upon the window-sill
A dusty book he spied, whose coat,
Like the Scotch miller's powdered twill,
The mealy owner might denote.
Called off from reading, unaware
The miller e'en had left it there.
A book all but forsaken now
For more advanced ones not so frank,
Nor less in vogue and taking rank ;
And yet it never shall outgrow
That infamy it first incurred,
Though—viewed in light which moderns know—
Capricious infamy absurd.
    The blunt straightforward Saxon tone,
Workaday language, even his own,
The sturdy thought, not deep but clear,
The hearty unbelief sincere,
Arrested him much like a hand
Clapped on the shoulder.   Here he found
Body to doubt, rough standing-ground.
After some pages brief were scanned,
' Wilt loan me this ? ' he anxious said.
The shrewd Scot turned his square, strong
    head—
The book he saw, in troubled trim,
Fearing for Nathan, even him
So young, and for the mill, may be,
Should his unspoken heresy

Get bruited so.   The lad but part
Might penetrate that senior heart.
Vainly the miller would dissuade ;
Pledge gave he, and the loan was made.

    Reclined that night by candle dim
He read, then slept, and woke afraid :
The White Hill's slide ! the Indian skull !
But this wore off ; and unto him
Came acquiescence, which tho' dull
Was hardly peace.   An altered earth
Sullen he tilled, in Adam's frame
When thrust from Eden out to dearth
And blest no more, and wise in shame.
The fall ! nor aught availed at need
To Nathan, not each filial deed
Done for his mother, to allay
This ill.   But tho' the Deist's sway,
Broad as the prairie fire, consumed
Some pansies which before had bloomed
Within his heart ; it did but feed
To clear the soil for upstart weed.

    Yes, ere long came replacing mood.
The god, expelled from given form,
Went out into the calm and storm.
Now, ploughing near the isles of wood
In dream he felt the loneness come,
In dream regarded there the loam
Turned first by him.   Such mental food
Need quicken, and in natural way,
Each germ of Pantheistic sway,
Whose influence, nor always drear,
Tenants our maiden hemisphere ;
As if, dislodged long since from cells
Of Thracian woodlands, hither stole—
Hither, to renew their old control—

Pan and the pagan oracles.

How frequent when Favonius low
Breathed from the copse which mild did wave
Over his father's sylvan grave,
And stirred the corn, he stayed the hoe,
And leaning, listening, felt a thrill
Which heathenised against the will.

Years sped.   But years attain not truth,
Nor length of life avails at all ;
But time instead contributes ruth :
His mother—her the garners call :
When sicklemen with sickles go,
The churl of nature reaps her low.

Let now the breasts of Ceres swell—
In shooks, with golden tassels gay,
The Indian corn its trophies ray
About the log-house ; is it well
With death's ripe harvest ?—To believe,
Belief to win nor more to grieve !
But how ? a sect about him stood
In thin and scattered neighbourhood ;
Uncanny, and in rupture new ;
Nor were all lives of members true
And good.   For them who hate and heave
Contempt on rite and creed sublime,
Yet to their own rank fable cleave—
Abject, the latest shame of time ;
These quite repelled, for still his mind
Erring, was of no vulgar kind.
Alone, and at Doubt's freezing pole
He wrestled with the pristine forms
Like the first man.   By inner storms
Held in solution, so his soul
Ripened for hour of such control

As shapes, concretes. The influence came,
And from a source that well might claim
Surprise.
        'Twas in a lake-port new,
A mart for grain, by chance he met
A Jewess who about him threw
Else than Nerea's amorous net
And dubious wile. 'Twas Miriam's race :
A sibyl breathed in Agar's grace—
A sibyl, but a woman too ;
He felt her grateful as the rains
To Rephaim and the Rama plains
In drought. Ere won, herself did woo :
' Wilt join my people ? ' Love is power ;
Came the strange plea in yielding hour.
Nay, and turn Hebrew ? But why not ?
If backward still the inquirer goes
To get behind man's present lot
Of crumbling faith ; for rear-wall shows
Far behind Rome and Luther—what ?
The crag of Sinai. Here then plant
Thyself secure : 'tis adamant.
      Still as she dwelt on Zion's story
He felt the glamour, caught the gleam ;
All things but these seemed transitory—
Love, and his love's Jerusalem.
And interest in a mitred race,
With awe which to the fame belongs,
These in receptive heart found place
When Agar chanted David's songs.
      'Twas passion. But the Puritan—
Mixed latent in his blood—a strain
How evident, of Hebrew source ;
'Twas that, diverted here in force,
Which biased—hardly might do less.

Hereto append, how earnestness,
Which disbelief for first-fruits bore,
Now, in recoil, by natural stress
Constrained to faith—to faith in more
Than prior disbelief had spurned ;
As if, when he toward credence turned,
Distance therefrom but gave career
For impetus that shot him sheer
Beyond. Agar rejoiced ; nor knew
How such a nature, charged with zeal,
Might yet overpass that limit due
Observed by her. For woe or weal
They wedded, one in heart and creed.
Transferring fields with title-deed,
From rustic life he quite withdrew—
Traded, and throve. Two children came :
Sedate his heart, nor sad the dame.
But years subvert ; or he outgrew
(While yet confirmed in all the myth)
The mind infertile of the Jew.
His northern nature, full of pith,
Vigour and enterprise and will,
Having taken thus the Hebrew bent,
Might not abide inactive so
And but the empty forms fulfil :
Needs utilise the mystic glow—
For nervous energies find vent.

    The Hebrew seers announce in time
The return of Judah to her prime ;
Some Christians deemed it then at hand.
Here was an object : Up and do !
With seed and tillage help renew—
Help reinstate the Holy Land.

    Some zealous Jews on alien soil
Who still from Gentile ways recoil,

And loyally maintain the dream,
Salute upon the Paschal day
With *Next year in Jerusalem !*
Now Nathan turning unto her,
Greeting his wife at morning ray,
Those words breathed on the Passover ;
But she, who mutely startled lay,
In the old phrase found import new,
In the blithe tone a bitter cheer
That did the very speech subdue.
She kenned her husband's mind austere,
Had watched his reveries grave ; he meant
No flourish mere of sentiment.
Then what to do ? or how to stay ?
Decry it ? that would faith unsay.
Withstand him ? but she gently loved.
And so with Agar here it proved,
As oft it may, the hardy will
Overpowered the deep monition still.

Enough ; fair fields and household charms
They quit, sell all, and cross the main
With Ruth and a young child in arms.
A tract secured on Sharon's plain,
Some sheds he built, and ground walled in
Defensive ; toil severe but vain.
The wandering Arabs, wonted long
(Nor crime they deemed it, crime nor sin)
To scale the desert convents strong—
In sly foray leaped Nathan's fence
And robbed him ; and no recompense
Attainable where law was none
Or perjured. Resolute hereon,
Agar, with Ruth and the young child,
He lodged within the stronghold town

Of Zion, and his heart exiled
To abide the worst on Sharon's lea.
Himself and honest servants three
Armed husbandmen became, as erst
His sires in Pequod wilds immersed.
Hittites—foes pestilent to God
His fathers old those Indians deemed :
Nathan the Arabs here esteemed
The same—slaves meriting the rod ;
And out he spake it ; which bred hate
The more imperilling his state.

    With muskets now his servants slept :
Alternate watch and ward they kept
In grounds beleaguered.   Not the less
Visits at stated times he made
To them in Zion's walled recess.
Agar with sobs of suppliance prayed
That he would fix there : ' Ah, for good
Tarry ! abide with us, thine own ;
Put not these blanks between us ; should
Such space be for a shadow thrown ?
Quit Sharon, husband ; leave to brood ;
Serve God by cleaving to thy wife,
Thy children.   If come fatal strife—
Which I forebode—nay ! ' and she flung
Her arms about him there, and clung.

    She plead.   But tho' his heart could feel,
'Twas mastered by inveterate zeal.
Even the nursling's death ere long
Balked not his purpose tho' it wrung.

    But Time the cruel, whose smooth way
Is feline, patient for the prey
That to this twig of being clings ;
And Fate, which from her ambush springs

And drags the loiterer soon or late
Unto a sequel unforeseen ;
These doomed him and cut short his date ;
But first was modified the lien
The husband had on Agar's heart ;
And next a prudence slid athwart—
After distrust.   But be unsaid
That steep toward which the current led.
Events shall speak.
               And now the guide,
Who did in sketch this tale begin,
Parted with Clarel at the inn ;
And ere long came the eventide.

XVIII

NIGHT

LIKE sails convened when calms delay
Off the twin forelands on fair day,
So, on Damascus' plain behold
Mid groves and gardens, girdling ones,
White fleets of sprinkled villas, rolled
In the green ocean of her environs.
    There when no minaret receives
The sun that gilds yet St. Sophia,
Which loath and later it bereaves,
The peace fulfils the heart's desire.
In orchards mellowed by eve's ray
The prophet's son in turban green,
Mild, with a patriarchal mien,
Gathers his fruity spoil. In play
Of hide-and-seek where alleys be,
The branching Eden brooks ye see
Peeping, and fresh as on the day
When haply Abram's steward went—
Mild Eliezer, musing, say—
By those same banks, to join the tent
In Canaan pitched. From Hermon stray
Cool airs that in a dream of snows
Temper the ardour of the rose ;
While yet to moderate and reach
A tone beyond our human speech,
How steals from cloisters of the groves
The *ave* of the vesper-doves.

Such notes, translated into hues,
Thy wall, Angelico, suffuse,
Whose tender pigments melt from view—
Die down, die out, as sunsets do.

    But rustling trees aloft entice
To many a house-top, old and young :
Aerial people ! see them throng ;
And the moon comes up from Paradise.

    But in Jerusalem—not there
Loungers at eve to roof repair
So frequent. Haply two or three
Small quiet groups far off you see,
Or some all uncompanioned one
(Like ship-boy at mast-head alone)
Watching the star-rise. Silently
So Clarel stands, his vaulted room
Opening upon a terrace free,
Lifted above each minor dome
On grade beneath. Glides, glides away
The twilight of the Wailing Day.
The apostate's story fresh in mind,
Fain Clarel here had mused thereon,
But more upon Ruth's lot, so twined
With clinging ill. But every thought
Of Ruth was strangely underrun
By Celio's image. Celio—sought
Vainly in body—now appeared
As in the spiritual part,
Haunting the air, and in the heart.
    Back to his chamber Clarel veered,
Seeking that alms which unrest craves
Of slumber : alms withheld from him ;
For midnight, rending all her graves,
Showed in a vision far and dim

Still Celio—and in pallid stress
Fainting amid contending press
Of shadowy fiends and cherubim.
Later, anew he sought the roof ;
And started, for not far aloof,
He caught some dubious object dark,
Huddled and hooded, bowed, and set
Under the breast-high parapet,
And glimmering with a dusky spark.
It moved, it murmured.   In deep prayer
'Twas Abdon under *talith*.   Rare
That scarf of supplication—old,
Of India stuff, with braid of gold
In cipher.   Did the Black Jew keep
The saying—*Prayer is more than sleep ?*
Islam says that.   The Hebrew rose,
And, kindled by the starry sky,
In broidered text that mystic flows
The *talith* gleams.   Divested then
He turned, not knowing Clarel nigh,
And would have passed him all unseen.
But Clarel spake.   It roused annoy—
An Eastern Jew in rapt employ
Spied by the Gentile.   But a word
Dispelled distrust, goodwill restored.
     ' Stay with me,' Clarel said ; ' go not.
A shadow, but I scarce know what—
It haunts me.   Is it presage ?—Hark !
That piercing cry from out the dark ! '
' 'Tis for some parted spirit—gone,
Just gone.   The custom of the town
That cry is ; yea, the watcher's breath
Instant upon the stroke of death.'
     ' Anew ! 'Tis like a tongue of flame
Shot from the fissure ' ; and stood still :

' Can fate the boding thus fulfil ?
First ever I, first to disclaim
Such premonitions.—Thrillest yet
'Tis over, but we might have met ?—
Hark, hark ; again the cry is sped ;
For *him* it is—found now—nay, fled ! '

XIX

THE FULFILMENT

Such passion !—But have hearts forgot
That ties may form where words be not ?
The spiritual sympathy
Transcends the social.   Which appears
In that presentiment, may be,
Of Clarel's inquietude of fears
Proved just.
           Yes, some retreat to win
Even more secluded than the court
The Terra Santa locks within :
Celio had found withdrawn resort
And lodging in the deeper town.
There, by a gasping ill distressed—
Such as attacks the hump-bowed one—
After three days the malady pressed :
He knew it, knew his course was run,
And, turning toward the wall, found rest.
      'Twas Syrians watched the parting hour—
And Syrian women shrilled the cry
That wailed it.   This, with added store,
Learned Clarel, putting all else by
To get at items of the dead.
Nor, in the throb that casts out fear,
Aught recked he of a scruple here ;
But, finding leaves that might bestead,
The jotted journaled thoughts he read.

A second self therein he found,
But stronger—with the heart to brave
All questions on that primal ground
Laid bare by faith's receding wave.
But lo, arrested in event—
Hurried down Hades' steep descent ;
Cut off while in progressive stage
Perchance, ere years might more unfold :
Who young dies, leaves life's tale half told.
How then ?   Is death the book's fly-page ?
Is no hereafter ?   If there be,
Death foots what record ? how forestalls
Acquittance in eternity ?
Advance too, and through age on age ?
Here the tree lies not as it falls ;
For howsoe'er in words of man
The word and will of God be feigned,
No incompletion 's heaven ordained.

    Clarel, through him these reveries ran.

XX

BEYOND the city's thin resort
And northward from the Ephraim port
The Vale of Ashes keepeth place.
If stream it have which showeth face,
Thence Kedron issues when in flood :
A pathless dell men seldom trace ;
The same which after many a rood
Down deepens by the city wall
Into a glen, where—if we deem
Joel's wild text no Runic dream—
An archangelic trump shall call
The nations of the dead from wreck,
Convene them in one judgment-hall
The hollow of Melchizedek.

    That upper glade by quarries old
Reserves for weary ones a seat—
Porches of caves, stone benches cold,
Grateful in sultry clime to meet.
To this secluded spot austere,
Priests bore—Talmudic records treat—
The ashes from the altar ; here
They laid them, hallowed in release,
Shielded from winds in glade of peace.

    From following the bier to end
Hitherward now see Clarel tend ;
A dell remote from Celio's mound,
As he for time would shun the ground

So freshly opened for the dead,
Nor linger there while aliens stray
And ceremonious gloom is shed.
    Withdrawing to this quiet bay
He felt a natural influence glide
In lenitive through every vein,
And reach the heart, lull heart and brain.
The comrade old was by his side,
And solace shared.   But this would pass,
Or dim eclipse would steal thereon,
As over autumn's hill-side grass
The cloud.   Howbeit, in freak anon
His Bible he would muttering con,
Then turn, and brighten with a start—
' I hear them, hear them in my heart ;
Yea, friend in Christ, I hear them swell—
The trumpets of Immanuel ! '
Illusion.   But in other hour
When oft he would foretell the flower
And sweets that time should yet bring in,
A happy world, with peace for dower—
This more of interest could win ;
For he, the solitary man
Who such a social dream could fan,
What had he known himself of bliss ?
And—nearing now his earthly end—
Even that he pledged he needs must miss.
    To Clarel now, such musings lend
A vague disturbance, as they wend
Returning thro' the noiseless glade.
But in the gate Nehemiah said,
' My room in court is pleasant, see ;
Not yet you 've been there—come with me.'

XXI

BY-PLACES

On Salem's surface undermined,
Lo, present alley, lane or wynd
Obscure, which pilgrims seldom gain
Or tread, who wonted guides retain.
Humble the pilots native there :
Following humbly need ye fare :
Afoot ; for never camels pass—
Camels, which elsewhere in the town,
Stalk through the street and brush the gown ;
Nor steed, nor mule, nor smaller ass.
Some by-paths, flanked by wall and wall,
Affect like glens.   Dismantled, torn,
Disastrous houses, ripe for fall—
Haggard as Horeb, or the rock
Named Hermit, antler of Cape Horn—
Shelter, in chamber grimed, or hall,
The bearded goat-herd's bearded flock ;
Or quite abandoned, sold to fear,
Yawn, and like plundered tombs appear.
Here, if alone, strive all ye can,
Needs must ye start at meeting man.
Yet man here harbours, even he—
Harbours like lizard in dry well,
Or stowaway in hull at sea
Down by the kelson ; criminal,
Or penitent, or wretch undone,
Or anchorite, or kinless one,

Or wight cast off by kin ; or soul
Which anguished from the hunter stole—
Like Emim Bey the Mameluke.
He—armed, and, happily, mounted well—
Leaped the inhuman citadel
In Cairo ; fled—yea, bleeding, broke
Through shouting lanes his breathless way
Into the desert ; nor at bay
Even there might stand ; but, fox-like, on,
And ran to earth in Zion's town ;
Here maimed, disfigured, crouched in den,
And crouching died—securest then.

    With these be hearts in each degree
Of craze, whereto some creed is key ;
Which, mastered by the awful myth,
Find here, on native soil, the pith ;
And leaving a shrewd world behind—
To trances open-eyed resigned—
As visionaries of the Word
Walk like somnambulists abroad.

XXII

THROUGH such retreats of dubious end
Behold the saint and student wend,
Stirring the dust that here may keep
Like that on mummies long asleep
In Theban tomb.   Those alleys passed,
A little square they win—a waste
Shut in by towers so hushed, so blind,
So tenantless and left forlorn
As seemed—an ill surmise was born
Of something prowling there behind.

    An arch, with keystone slipped half down
Like a dropped jaw—they enter that ;
Repulse nor welcome in the gate :
Climbed, and an upper chamber won.
It looked out through low window small
On other courts of bale shut in,
Whose languishment of crumbling wall
Breathed that despair alleged of sin.
Prediction and fulfilment met
In faint appealings from the rod :
Wherefore forever dost forget—
For so long time forsake, O God ?

    But Clarel turned him, heedful more
To note the place within.   The floor
Rudely was tiled ; and little there
A human harbour might express

Save a poor chest, a couch, a chair ;
A hermitage how comfortless.
The beams of the low ceiling bare
Were wreck-stuff from the Joppa strand :
Scant the live timber in that land.
Upon the cot the host sat down,
Short breathing, with late travel spent ;
And wiping beads from brow and crown,
Essayed a smile, in kindness meant.

But now a little foot was heard
Light coming.　On the hush it fell
Like tinkling of the camel-bell
In Uz.　' Hark !　yea, she comes—my bird ! '
Cried Nehemiah who hailed the hap ;
' Yea, friend in Christ, quick now ye 'll see
God's messenger which feedeth me ' ;
And rising to the expected tap,
He oped the door.　Alone was seen
Ruth with a napkin coarse yet clean,
Folding a loaf.　Therewith she bore
A water-pitcher, nothing more.
These alms, the snowy robe and free,
The veil which hid each tress from sight,
Might indicate a vestal white
Or priestess of sweet charity.

The voice was on the lip ;　but eyes
Arrested in their frank accost,
Checked speech, and looked in opening skies
Upon the stranger.　Said the host,
Easing her hands, ' Bird, bird, come in :
Well-doing never was a sin—
God bless thee ! '　In suffusion dim
His eyes filled.　She eluding him,
Retreated.　' What, and flown ? ' breathed he :
' Daily this raven comes to me ;

But what should make it now so shy ? '
The hermit motioned here to share
The loaf with Clarel ; who put by
The proffer.   So, with Crusoe air
Of castaway on isle in sea
Withdrawn, he broke the unshared bread—
But not before a blessing said :
Loaf in left hand, the right hand raised
Higher, and eyes which heavenward gazed.

    Ere long—refection done—the youth
Lured him to talk of things, in range
Linking themselves at last with Ruth.
Her sire he spake of.   Here 'twas strange
How o'er the enthusiast stole a change—
A meek superior look in sooth :
' Poor Nathan, did man ever stray
As thou ? to Judaise to-day !
To deem the crook of Christ shall yield
To Aaron's staff ! to till thy field
In hope that harvest-time shall see
Solomon's hook in golden glee
Reaping the ears.   Well, well ! meseems—
Heaven help him ; dreams, but dreams—dreams,
    dreams ! '
' But thou, thou too, with faith sincere
Surely believ'st in Jew restored.'
' Yea, as forerunner of our Lord.—
Poor man, he 's weak ; 'tis even here '—
Touching his forehead—' he 's amiss.'

    Clarel scarce found reply to this,
Conjecturing that Nathan too
Must needs hold Nehemiah in view
The same ; the which an after-day
Confirmed by proof.   But now from sway
Of thoughts he would not have recur,

He slid, and into dream of her
Who late within that cell shed light
Like the angel succourer by night
Of Peter dungeoned.   But apace
He turned him, for he heard the breath,
The old man's breath, in sleep.   The face,
Though tranced, struck not like trance of death
All rigid ; not a masque like that,
Iced o'er, which none may penetrate,
Conjecturing of aught below.
Death freezes, but sleep thaws.   And so
The inmate lay, some lines revealed—
Effaced, when life from sleep comes back.
And what their import ?   Be it sealed.
But Clarel felt as in affright
Did Eliphaz the Temanite
When passed the vision ere it spake.

    He stole forth, striving with his thought,
Leaving Nehemiah in slumber caught—
Alone, and in an unlocked room,
Safe as a stone in vacant tomb,
Stone none molest, for it is naught.

XXIII

THE CLOSE

NEXT day the wanderer drawing near
Saluting with his humble cheer,
Made Clarel start.   Where now the look
That face but late in slumber took ?
Had he but dreamed it ?   It was gone.
        But other thoughts were stirring soon,
To such good purpose, that the saint
Through promptings scarce by him divined,
Anew led Clarel thro' constraint
Of inner by-ways, yet inclined
Away from his peculiar haunt,
And came upon a little close,
One wall whereof a creeper won.
On casement sills, small pots in rows
Showed herb and flower, the shade and sun—
Surprise how blest in town but sere.
Low breathed the guide, ' They harbour here—
Agar, and my young raven, Ruth.
And, see, there 's Nathan, nothing loath,
Just in from Sharon, 'tis his day ;
And, yes—the Rabbi in delay.'—
        The group showed just within the door
Swung open where the creeper led.
In lap the petting mother bore
The half-reclining maiden's head—
The stool drawn neighbouring the chair ;
In front, erect, the father there,

Hollow in cheek, but rugged, brown—
Sharon's red soil upon his shoon—
With zealot gesture urged some plea
Which brought small joy to Agar's eyes,
Whereto turned Ruth's.   In scrutiny
Impassive, wrinkled, and how wise
(If wisdom be but craft profound)
Sat the hoar Rabbi.   This his guise :
In plaits a head-dress agate-bound,
A sable robe with mystic hem—
Clasps silver, locked in monogram.

An unextinguished lamp they view
Whose flame scarce visibly did sway,
Which having burned till morning dew
Might not be quenched on Saturday
The unaltered sabbath of the Jew.
Struck by the attitudes, the scene,
And loath, a stranger, to advance
Obtrusive, coming so between ;
While, in emotion new and strange,
Ruth thrilled him with life's first romance ;
Clarel abashed and faltering stood,
With cheek that knew a novel change.
But Nehemiah with air subdued
Made known their presence ; and Ruth turned,
And Agar also, and discerned
The stranger, and a settle placed :
Matron and maid with welcome graced
Both visitors, and seemed to find
In travel-talk which here ensued
Relief to burdens of the mind.
But by the sage was Clarel viewed
With stony and unfriendly look—
Fixed inquisition, hard to brook.

And that embarrassment he raised
The Rabbi marked, and colder gazed.
But in redemption from his glance—
For a benign deliverance—
On Clarel fell the virgin's eyes,
Pure home of all we seek and prize,
And crossing with their humid ray
The Levite's arid eyes of gray—
But skill is none to word the rest:
To Clarel's heart there came a swell
Like the first tide that ever pressed
Inland, and of a deep did tell.

Thereafter, little speech was had
Save syllables which do but skim;
Even in these, the zealot—made
A slave to one tyrannic whim—
Was scant; while still the sage unkind
Sat a torpedo-fish, with mind
Intent to paralyse, and so
Perchance, make Clarel straight forgo
Acquaintance with his flock, at least
With two, whose yearnings—he the priest
More than conjectured—oft did flow
Averse from Salem. None the less
A talismanic gentleness
Maternal welled from Agar faint;
Thro' the sad circle's ill constraint
Her woman's way could yet instil
Her prepossession, her goodwill;
And when at last they bade good-bye—
The visitors—another eye
Spake at the least of amity.

XXIV

THE GIBE

In the south wall, where low it creeps
Crossing the hollow down between
Moriah and Zion, by dust-heaps
Of rubbish in a lonely scene,
A little door there is, and mean—
Such as a stable may befit;
'Tis locked, nor do they open it
Except when days of drought begin,
To let the water-donkeys in
From Rogel. 'Tis in site the gate
Of Scripture named the dung-gate—that
Also (the legends this instil)
Through which from over Kedron's rill—
In fear of rescue should they try
The way less roundabout and shy—
By torch the tipstaves Jesus led,
And so thro' back-street hustling sped
To Pilate. Odour bad it has
This gate in story, and alas,
In fact as well, and is in fine
Like ancient Rome's port Esquiline
Wherefrom the scum was cast.—

                              Next day
Ascending Zion's rear, without
The wall, the saint and Clarel stay
Their feet, being hailed, and by a shout

From one who nigh the small gate stood :
' Ho, ho there, worthy pilgrims, ho !
Acquainted in this neighbourhood ?
What city 's this ? town beautiful
Of David ?   I 'm a stranger, know.
'Tis heavy prices here must rule ;
Choice house-lot now, what were it worth ?
How goes the market ? ' and more mirth.
    Down there into the place unclean
They peer, they see the man therein,
An iron-gray, short, rugged one,
Round-shouldered, and of knotty bone ;
A hammer swinging in his hand,
And pouch at side, by the ill door.
Him had they chanced upon before
Or rather at a distance seen
Upon the hills, with curious mien
And eyes that—scarce in pious dream
Or sad humility, 'twould seem—
Still earthward bent, would pry and pore.
Perceiving that he shocked the twain,
His head he wagged, and called again,
' What city 's this ? town beautiful——'
No more they heard ; but to annul
The cry, here Clarel quick as thought
Turned with the saint and refuge sought
Passing an angle of the wall.
    When now at slower pace they went
Clarel observed the sinless one
Turning his Bible-leaves content ;
And presently he paused : ' Dear son,
The Scripture is fulfilled this day ;
Note what these *Lamentations* say ;
The doom the prophet doth rehearse
In chapter second, fourteenth verse :

" *All that pass by clap their hands*
At thee ; they hiss, and wag the head,
Saying, Is this the city "—read,
Thyself here read it where it stands.'
    Inquisitive he quick obeyed,
Then dull relapsed, and nothing said,
Tho' more he mused, still labouring there
Upward, by arid gullies bare :—
What object sensible to touch
Or quoted fact may faith rely on,
If faith confideth overmuch
That here 's a monument in Zion :
Its substance ebbs—see, day and night
The sands subsiding from the height ;
In time, absorbed, these grains may help
To form new sea-bed, slug and kelp.
    ' The gate,' cried Nehemiah, ' the gate
Of David ! ' Wending thro' the strait,
And marking that, in common drought,
'Twas yellow waste within as out,
The student mused : The desert, see,
It parts not here, but silently,
Even like a leopard by our side,
It seems to enter in with us—
At home amid men's homes would glide.
But hark ! that wail how dolorous :
So grieve the souls in endless dearth ;
Yet sounds it human—of the earth !

XXV

HUTS

THE stone huts face the stony wall
Inside—the city's towering screen—
Leaving a reptile lane between ;
And streetward not a window small,
Cranny nor loophole least is seen :
Through excess of biting sympathies
So hateful to the people's eyes
Those lepers and their evil nook,
No outlook from it will they brook :
None enter ; condolence is none.
That lava glen in Luna's sphere,
More lone than any earthly one—
Whereto they Tycho's name have given—
Not more from visitant is riven
Than this stone lane.

                      But who crouch here ?
Have these been men ? these did men greet
As fellows once ?   It is a scene—
Illusion of time's mirage fleet :
On dry shard-heaps, and things which rot—
Scarce into weeds, for weeds are green—
Backs turned upon their den, they squat,
Some gossips of that tribe unclean.

    Time was when Holy Church did take,
Over lands then held by Baldwin's crown,
True care for such for Jesu's sake,

Who (so they read in ages gone)
Even as a leper was foreshown ;
And, tho' apart their lot she set,
It was with solemn service yet,
And forms judicial lent their tone :
The sick-mass offered, next was shed
Upon the afflicted human one
The holy water. He was led
Unto the house aloof, his home
Thenceforth. And here, for type of doom,
Some cemetery dust was thrown
Over his head : ' Die to the world :
Her wings of hope and fear be furled :
Brother, live now to God alone.'
And from the people came the chant :
' *My soul is troubled, joy is curbed,*
All my bones they are disturbed ;
God, Thy strength and mercy grant ! '
And next, in order due, the priest
Each habit and utensil blessed—
Hair-cloth and barrel, clapper, glove ;
And one by one as these were given,
With law's dread charge pronounced in love,
So, link by link, life's chain was riven—
The leper faded in remove.
　　The dell of isolation here
To match, console, and (could man prove
More than a man) in part endear,
How well had come that smothered text
Which Julian's pagan mind hath vexed—
And ah, for soul that finds it clear :
' *He lives forbid ;*
From him our faces have we hid ;
No heart desires him, none redress,
He hath nor form nor comeliness ;

For a transgressor he 's suspected,
Behold, he is a thing infected,
Smitten of God, by men rejected.'
    But otherwise the ordinance flows.
For, moving toward the allotted cell,
Beside the priest the leper goes :
' I 've chosen it, here will I dwell.'
He 's left.   At gate the priest puts up
A cross, a can ;   therein doth drop
The first small alms, which laymen swell.
To aisles returned, the people kneel ;
Heart-piercing suppliance—appeal.

    But not the austere maternal care
When closed the ritual, ended there
With benediction.   Yet to heal,
Rome did not falter, could not faint ;
She prompted many a tender saint,
Widow or virgin ministrant.
But chiefly may Sybella here
In chance citation fitly show,
Countess who under Zion's brow
In house of St. John Almoner
Tended the cripples many a year.

    Tho' long from Europe's clime be gone
That pest which in the perished age
Could tendance such in love engage,
Still in the East the rot eats on.
Natheless the Syrian leper goes
Unfriended, save that man bestows
(His eye averting) chanceful pence
Then turns, and shares disgust of sense.

    Bonds sympathetic bind these three—
Faith, Reverence, and Charity.
If Faith once fail, the faltering mood
Affects—need must—the sisterhood.

XXVI

THE GATE OF ZION

As Clarel entered with the guide,
Beset they were by that sad crew—
With inarticulate clamour plied ;
And faces, yet defacements too,
Appealed to them ; but could not give
Expression.   There, still sensitive,
Our human nature, deep inurned
In voiceless visagelessness, yearned.
　　Behold, proud worm (if such can be),
What yet may come, yea, even to thee.
Who knoweth ? canst forecast the fate
In infinite ages ?   Probe thy state :
Sinless art thou ?   Then these sinned not.
These, these are men ; and thou art—what ?
　　For Clarel, turning in affright,
Fain would his eyes renounce the light.
But Nehemiah held on his path
Mild and unmoved—scarce seemed to heed
The suitors, or deplore the scath—
His soul preoccupied and freed
From actual objects thro' the sway
Of visionary scenes intense—
The wonders of a mystic day
And Zion's old magnificence.
Nor hither had he come to show
The leper-huts, but only so
To visit once again the hill
And gate Davidic.

In ascent
They win the port's high battlement,
And thence in sweep they view at will
That theatre of heights which hold
As in a Coliseum's fold
The guarded Zion.   They command
The Mount of Solomon's Offence,
The Crag of Evil Council, and
Iscariot's gallows-eminence.

Pit too they mark where long ago
Dull fires of refuse, shot below,
The city's litter, smouldering burned,
Clouding the glen with smoke impure,
And griming the foul shapes obscure
Of dismal chain-gangs in their shame
Raking the garbage thither spurned :
Tophet the place—transferred, in name,
To penal Hell.

But shows there naught
To win here a redeeming thought ?
Yes : welcome in its nearer seat
The white Cœnaculum they greet,
Where still an upper room is shown—
In dream avouched the very one
Wherein the Supper first was made
And Christ those words of parting said,
Those words of love by loved St. John
So tenderly recorded.   Ah,
They be above us like a star,
Those Paschal words.

But they descend ;
And as within the wall they wend,
A Horror hobbling on low crutch
Draws near, but still refrains from touch.
Before the saint in low estate

He fawns, who with considerate
Mild glance regards him.   Clarel shrank :
And he, is *he* of human rank ?—
' Knowest thou him ? ' he asked.—' Yea, yea,'
And beamed on that disfeatured clay :
' Toulib, to me ? to Him are due
These thanks—the God of me and you
And all ; to whom His own shall go
In Paradise and be reclad,
Transfigured like the morning glad.—
Yea, friend in Christ, this man I know,
This fellow-man.'—And afterward
The student from true sources heard
How Nehemiah had proved his friend,
Sole friend even of that trunk of woe,
When sisters failed him in the end.

MATRON AND MAID

Days fleet.   No vain enticements lure
Clarel to Agar's roof.   Her tact
Prevailed : the Rabbi might not act
His will austere.   And more and more
A prey to one devouring whim,
Nathan yet more absented him.
Welcome the matron ever had
For Clarel.   Was the youth not one
New from the clime she doated on ?
And if indeed an exile sad
By daisy in a letter laid
Reminded be of home-delight,
Tho' there first greeted by the sight
Of that transmitted flower—how then
Not feel a kin emotion bred
At glimpse of face of countryman
Tho' stranger ?   Yes, a Jewess—born
In Gentile land where nature's wreath
Exhales the first creation's breath—
The waste of Judah made her lorn.
The student, sharing not her blood,
Nearer in tie of spirit stood
Than he she called Rabboni.   So
In Agar's liking did he grow—
Deeper in heart of Ruth ; and learned
The more how both for freedom yearned ;
And much surmised, too, left unsaid
By the tried mother and the maid.

Howe'er dull natures read the signs
Where untold grief a hermit pines—
The anxious, strained, weak, nervous air
Of trouble, which like shame may wear
Her gaberdine ; though soul in feint
May look pathetic self-restraint,
For ends pernicious ; real care,
Sorrow made dumb where duties move,
Never eluded love, true love,
A deep diviner.
     Here, for space
The past of wife and daughter trace.
Of Agar's kin for many an age
Not one had seen the heritage
Of Judah ; Gentile lands detained.
So, while they clung to Moses' lore
Far from the land his guidance gained,
'Twas Eld's romance, a treasured store
Like plate inherited.   In fine
It graced, in seemly way benign,
That family feeling of the Jew,
Which hallowed by each priestly rite,
Makes home a temple—sheds delight
Naomi ere her trial knew.
  Happy was Agar ere the seas
She crossed for Zion.   Pride she took—
Pride, if in small felicities—
Pride in her little court, a nook
Where morning-glories starred the door :
So sweet without, so snug within.
At sunny matin meal serene
Her damask cloth she 'd note.   It bore
In Hebrew text about the hem,
Mid broidered cipher and device,
' IF I FORGET THEE, O JERUSALEM ! '

And swam before her humid eyes,
In rainbowed distance, Paradise.
Faith, ravished, followed Fancy's path
In more of bliss than nature hath.
But ah, the dream to test by deed,
To seek to handle the ideal
And make a sentiment serve need :
To try to realise the unreal !
'Twas not that Agar reasoned—nay,
She did but feel, true woman's way.
What solace from the desert win
Far from known friends, familiar kin ?
How nearer God ?   The chanted Zion
Showed graves, but graves to gasp and die on.
    Nathan, her convert, for his sake
Grief had she stifled long ; but now,
The nursling one lay pale and low.
Oft of that waxen face she 'd think
Beneath the stones ; her heart would sink
And in hard bitterness repine,
' Slim grass, poor babe, to grave of thine ! '

    Ruth, too, when here a child she came,
Would blurt in reckless childhood's way,
' 'Tis a bad place.'   But the sad dame
Would check ; and, as the maiden grew
Counsel she kept—too much she knew.
But how to give her feelings play ?
With cherished pots of herbs and flowers
She strove to appease the hungry hours ;
Each leaf bedewed with many a tear
For Gentile land, how green and dear !
What tho' the dame and daughter both
In synagogue, behind the grate
Dividing sexes, oft-times sate ?

It was with hearts but chill and loath ;
Never was heaven served by that
Cold form.—With Clarel seemed to come
A waftage from the fields of home,
Crossing the wind from Judah's sand,
Reviving Agar, and of power
To make the bud in Ruth expand
With promise of unfolding hour.

XXVIII

TOMB AND FOUNTAIN

CLAREL and Ruth—might it but be
That range they could green uplands free
By gala orchards, when they fling
Their bridal favours, buds of Spring ;
And, dreamy in her morning swoon,
The lady of the night, the moon,
Looks pearly as the blossoming ;
And youth and nature's fond accord
Wins Eden back, that tales abstruse
Of Christ, the crucified, Pain's Lord,
Seem foreign—forged—incongruous.

Restrictions of that Eastern code
Immured the maiden. From abode
Frequent nor distant she withdrew
Except with Jewess, scarce with Jew.
So none the less in former mode,
Nehemiah still with Clarel went,
Who grew in liking and content
In company of one whose word
Babbled of Ruth—' My bird—God's bird.'

The twain were one mild morning led
Out to a waste where beauty clings,
Vining a grot how doubly dead :
The rifled *Sepulchre of Kings.*

Hewn from the rock a sunken space
Conducts to garlands—fit for vase—
In sculptured frieze above a tomb :
Palm leaves, pine-apples, grapes.   These bloom,
Involved in dearth—to puzzle us—
As 'twere thy line, Theocritus,
Dark Joel's text of terror threading :
Yes, strange that Pocahontas-wedding
Of contraries in old belief—
Hellenic cheer, Hebraic grief.
The homicide Herods, men aver,
Inurned behind that wreathage were.

But who is he uncovered seen,
Profound in shadow of the tomb
Reclined, with meditative mien
Intent upon the tracery ?
A low wind waves his Lydian hair :
A funeral man, yet richly fair—
Fair as the sabled violets be.
The frieze and this secluded one,
Retaining each a separate tone,
Beauty yet harmonised in grace
And contrast to the barren place.
But noting that he was discerned,
Salute the stranger made, then turned
And shy passed forth in obvious state
Of one who would keep separate.

Those cells explored, thro' dale they paced
Downward, and won Moriah's walls
And seated them.   Clarel recalls
The colonnades that Herod traced—
Herod, magnific Idumæan—
In marble along the mountain flank :

Column on column, rank on rank
Above the valley Tyropœon.
    Eastward, in altitude they view
Across Jehoshaphat, a crag
Of sepulchres and huts.   Thereto
They journey.   But awhile they lag
Beneath, to mark the tombs in row
Pierced square along the gloomy steep
In beetling broadside, and with show
Of port-holes in black battleship.
    They climb ; and Clarel turning saw
Their late resort, the hill of law—
Moriah, above the Kedron's bed ;
And, turreting his aged head,
The angle of King David's wall—
Acute seen here, here too best scanned,
As 'twere that cliff, tho' not so tall,
Nor tempest-sculptured therewithal,
Envisaged in Franconian land,
The marvel of the Pass.
                    Anon
A call he hears behind, in note
Familiar, being man's ; remote
No less, and strange in hollowed tone
As 'twere a voice from out the tomb.
A tomb it is ; and he in gloom
Of porch there biddeth them begone.
Clings to his knee a toddling one
Bewildered poising in wee hand
A pictured page—Nehemiah's boon—
He passive in the sun at stand.
Morosely then the Arab turns,
Snatches the gift, and drops and spurns.
    As down now from the crag they wend
Reverted glance see Clarel lend :

Thou guest of Death, which in his house
Sleep'st nightly, mayst thou not espouse
His daughter, Peace ?
                                        Aslant they come
Where, hid in shadow of the rocks,
Stone steps descend unto Siloam.
Proof to the fervid noonday tide
Reflected from the glen's steep side,
Moist ledge with ledge here interlocks,
Vaulting a sunken grotto deep.
    Down there, as quiet as in sleep,
Anew the stranger they descried
Sitting upon a step full low,
Watching the fountain's troubled tide
Which after ebb began to flow,
Gurgling from viewless caves.   The lull
Broke by the flood is wonderful.
Science explains it.   Bides no less
The true, innate mysteriousness.
Through him there might the vision flit
Of angel in Bethesda's pool
With porches five, so troubling it
That whoso bathed then was made whole ?
Or, by an equal dream beguiled,
Did he but list the fountain moan
Like Ammon's in the Libyan wild,
For muse and oracle both gone ?
    By chance a jostled pebble there
Slipped from the surface down the stair.
It jarred—it broke the brittle spell :
Siloam was but a rural well.

    Clarel who could again but shun
To obtrude on the secluded one,
Turned to depart.—' Ere yet we go,'

Said Nehemiah, ' I will below :
Dim be mine eyes, more dim they grow :
I 'll wash them in these waters cool,
As did the blind the Master sent,
And who came seeing from this pool ' ;
And down the grotto-stairs he went.

    The stranger, just ascending, stood ;
And, as the votary laved his eyes,
He marked, looked up, and Clarel viewed,
And they exchanged quick sympathies
Though but in glance, moved by that act
Of one whose faith transfigured fact.
A bond seemed made between them there ;
And presently the trio fare
Over Kedron, and in one accord
Of quietude and chastened tone
Approach the spot, tradition's own,
For ages held the garden of Our Lord.

XXIX

THE RECLUSE

Ere yet they win that verge and line,
Reveal the stranger.   Name him—Vine.
His home to tell—kin, tribe, estate—
Would naught avail.   Alighting grow,
As on the tree the mistletoe,
All gifts unique.   In seeds of fate
Borne on the winds these emigrate
And graft the stock.
               Vine's manner shy
A clog, a hindrance might imply ;
A lack of parlour-wont.   But grace
Which is in substance deep and grain
May, peradventure, well pass by
The polish of veneer.   No trace
Of passion's soil or lucre's stain,
Though life was now half-ferried o'er.
If use he served not, but forbore—
Such indolence might still but pine
In dearth of rich incentive high :
Apollo slave in Mammon's mine ?
Better Admetus' shepherd lie.

   A charm of subtle virtue shed
A personal influence coveted,
Whose source was difficult to tell
As ever was that perfumed spell
Of Paradise-flowers invisible
Which angels round Cecilia bred.

A saint then do we here unfold ?
Nay, the ripe flush, Venetian mould
Evinced no nature saintly fine,
But blood like swart Vesuvian wine.
What cooled the current ?   Under cheer
Of opulent softness, reigned austere
Control of self.   Flesh, but scarce pride,
Was curbed : desire was mortified ;
But less indeed by moral sway
Than doubt if happiness thro' clay
Be reachable.   No sackclothed man ;
Howbeit, in sort Carthusian
Tho' born a Sybarite.   And yet
Not beauty might he all forget,
The beauty of the world, and charm :
He prized it tho' it scarce might warm.
　　　Like to the nunnery's denizen
His virgin soul communed with men
But thro' the wicket.   Was it clear
This coyness bordered not on fear—
Fear or an apprehensive sense ?
Not wholly seemed it diffidence
Recluse.   Nor less did strangely wind
Ambiguous elfishness behind
All that : an Ariel unknown.
It seemed his very speech in tone
Betrayed disuse.   Thronged streets astir
To Vine but ampler cloisters were.
Cloisters ?   No monk he was, allow ;
But gleamed the richer for the shade
About him, as in sombre glade
Of Virgil's wood the Sibyl's Golden Bough.

XXX

AND wherefore by the convents be
Gardens ?   Ascetics roses twine ?
Nay, but there is a memory.
Within a garden walking see
The angered God.   And where the vine
And olive in the darkling hours
Inweave green sepulchres of bowers—
Who, to defend us from despair,
Pale undergoes the Passion there
In solitude ?   Yes, memory
Links Eden and Gethsemane ;
So that not meaningless in sway
Gardens adjoin the convents gray.

On Salem's hill in Solomon's years
Of gala, O the happy town !
In groups the people sauntered down,
And, Kedron crossing, lightly wound
Where now the tragic grove appears,
Then palmy, and a pleasure-ground.

The student and companions win
The wicket—pause, and enter in.
By roots strapped down in fold on fold—
Gnarled into wens and knobs and knees—
In olives, monumental trees,
The Pang's survivors they behold.

117

A wizened blue fruit drops from them,
Nipped harvest of Jerusalem.
Wistful here Clarel turned toward Vine,
And would have spoken ; but as well
Hail Dathan swallowed in the mine—
Tradition, legend, lent such spell
And rapt him in remoteness so.

    Meanwhile, in shade the olives throw,
Nehemiah pensive sat him down
And turned the chapter in St. John.

    What frame of mind may Clarel woo ?
He the night-scene in picture drew—
The band which came for sinless blood
With swords and staves, a multitude.
They brush the twigs, small birds take wing,
The dead boughs crackle, lanterns swing,
Till lo, they spy them thro' the wood.
' Master ! '—'Tis Judas.   Then the kiss.
And He, He falters not at this—
Speechless, unspeakably submiss :
The fulsome serpent on the cheek
Sliming : endurance more than meek—
Endurance of the fraud foreknown,
And fiend-heart in the human one.
Ah, now the pard on Clarel springs :
The Passion's narrative plants stings.

    To break away, he turns and views
The white-haired under olive bowed
Immersed in Scripture ; and he woos—
' Whate'er the chapter, read aloud.'
The saint looked up, but with a stare
Absent and wildered, vacant there.

    As part to kill time, part for task,
Some shepherd old pores over book—
Shelved farm-book of his life forepast

When he bestirred him and amassed ;
If chance one interrupt, and ask—
What read you ? he will turn a look
Which shows he knows not what he reads,
Or knowing, he but weary heeds,
Or scarce remembers ; here much so
With Nehemiah, dazed out and low.
And presently—to intercept—
Over Clarel, too, strange numbness crept.

A monk, custodian of the ground,
Drew nigh, and showed him by the steep
The rock or legendary mound
Where James and Peter fell asleep.
Dully the pilgrim scanned the spot,
Nor spake.—' Signor, and think'st thou not
'Twas sorrow brought their slumber on ?
St. Luke avers no sluggard rest :
Nay, but excess of feeling pressed
Till ache to apathy was won.'
To Clarel 'twas no hollow word.
Experience did proof afford.
For Vine, aloof he loitered—shrunk
In privity and shunned the monk.
Clarel awaited him.   He came—
The shadow of his previous air
Merged in a settled neutral frame—
Assumed, may be.   Would Vine disclaim
All sympathy the youth might share ?

About to leave, they turn to look
For him but late estranged in book :
Asleep he lay ; the face bent down
Viewless between the crossing arms,
One slack hand on the good book thrown
In peace that every care becharms.

Then died the shadow off from Vine :
A spirit seemed he not unblest
As here he made a quiet sign
Unto the monk : Spare to molest ;
Let this poor dreamer take his rest,
His fill of rest.
              But now at stand
Who there alertly glances up
By grotto of the Bitter Cup—
Spruce, and with volume light in hand
Bound smartly, late in reference scanned ?
Inquisitive Philistine : lo,
Tourists replace the pilgrims so.
    At peep of that brisk dapper man
Over Vine's face a ripple ran
Of freakish mockery, elfin light ;
Whereby what thing may Clarel see ?
O angels, rescue from the sight !
Paul Pry ? and in Gethsemane ?
He shrunk the thought of it to fan ;
Nor liked the freak in Vine that threw
Such a suggestion into view ;
Nor less it hit that fearful man.

XXXI

THE hill above the garden here
They rove ; and chance ere long to meet
A second stranger, keeping cheer
Apart.   Trapper or pioneer
He looked, astray in Judah's seat—
Or one who might his business ply
On waters under tropic sky.
Perceiving them as they drew near,
He rose, removed his hat to greet,
Disclosing so in shapely sphere
A marble brow over face embrowned :
So Sunium by her fane is crowned.
One read his superscription clear—
A genial heart, a brain austere—
And further, deemed that such a man
Though given to study, as might seem,
Was no scholastic partisan
Or euphonist of Academe,
But supplemented Plato's theme
With dædal life in boats and tents,
A messmate of the elements ;
And yet, more bronzed in face than mind,
Sensitive still and frankly kind—
Too frank, too unreserved, may be,
And indiscreet in honesty.
        But what implies the tinge of soil—
Like tarnish on Pizarro's spoil,

Precious in substance rudely wrought,
Peruvian plate—which here is caught ?
What means this touch of the untoward
In aspect hinting nothing froward ?

From Baalbec, for a new sojourn,
To Jewry Rolfe had made return ;
To Jewry's inexhausted shore
Of barrenness, where evermore
Some lurking thing he hoped to gain—
Slip quite behind the parrot-lore
Conventional, and—what attain ?
Struck by each clear or latent sign
Expressive in the stranger's air,
The student glanced from him to Vine :
Peers, peers—yes, needs that these must pair.
Clarel was young. In promise fine,
To him here first were brought together
Exceptional natures, of a weather
Strange as the tropics with strange trees,
Strange birds, strange fishes, skies and seas,
To one who in some meagre land
His bread wins by the horny hand.
What now may hap ? what outcome new
Elicited by contact true—
Frank, cordial contact of the twain ?
Crude wonderment, and proved but vain.
If average mortals social be,
And yet but seldom truly meet,
Closing like halves of apple sweet—
How with the rarer in degree ?
The informal salutation done,
Vine into his dumb castle went—
Not as all parley he would shun,
But looking down from battlement,

Ready, if need were, to accord
Reception to the other's word—
Nay, far from wishing to decline,
And neutral not without design,
May be.—
    ' Look, by Christ's belfry set,
Appears the Moslem minaret ! '
So—to fill trying pause alone—
Cried Rolfe ; and o'er the deep defile
Of Kedron, pointed toward the town,
Where, thronged about by many a pile
Monastic, but no vernal bower,
The Saracen shaft and Norman tower
In truce stand guard beside that Dome
Which canopies the Holy's home :
' The tower looks lopped ; it shows forlorn—
A stunted oak whose crown is shorn ;
But see, palm-like the minaret stands
Superior, and the tower commands.'
  ' Yon shaft,' said Clarel, ' seems ill-placed.'
' Ay, *seems* ; but 'tis for memory based.
The story 's known : how Omar there
After the town's surrender meek—
Hallowed to him, as dear to Greek—
Clad in his clouts of camel's hair,
And with the Patriarch robed and fine
Walking beneath the dome divine,
When came the Islam hour for prayer
Declined to use the carpet good
Spread for him in the church, but stood
Without, even yonder where is set
The monumental minaret ;
And, earnest in true suppliance cried,
Smiting his chest : " Me overrule !
Allah, to me be merciful ! "

'Twas little shared he victor-pride
Though victor. So the church he saved
Of purpose from that law engraved
Which prompt transferred to Allah sole
Each fane where once his rite might roll.
Long afterward, the town being stormed
By Christian knights, how ill conformed
The butchery then to Omar's prayer
And heart magnanimous.   But spare.'

    Response they looked ; and thence he warmed :
' Yon gray Cathedral of the Tomb,
Who reared it first ? a woman weak,
A second Mary, first to seek
In pagan darkness which had come,
The place where they had laid the Lord :
Queen Helena, she traced the site,
And cleared the ground, and made it bright
With all that zeal could then afford.
But Constantine—there falls the blight !
The mother's warm emotional heart,
Subserved it still the son's cold part ?
Even he who, timing well the tide,
Laced not the Cross upon Rome's flag
Supreme, till Jove began to lag
Behind the new religion's stride.
And Helena—ah, may it be
The saint herself not quite was free
From that which in the years bygone,
Made certain stately dames of France,
Such as the fair De Maintenon,
To string their rosaries of pearl,
And found brave chapels—sweet romance :
Coquetry of the borrowed curl ?—
You let me prate.'

'Nay, nay—go on,'
Cried Clarel, yet in such a tone
It showed disturbance.—
                  'Laud the dame :
Her church, admit, no doom it fears.
Unquelled by force of battering years—
Years, years and sieges, sword and flame ;
Fallen—rebuilt, to fall anew ;
By armies shaken, earthquake too ;
Lo, it abides—if not the same,
In selfsame spot.   Last time 'twas burnt
The Rationalist a lesson learnt.
But you know all.'—
                 'Nay, not the end,'
Said Vine.   And Clarel, 'We attend.'
   'Well, on the morrow never shrunk
From wonted rite the steadfast monk,
Though hurt and even maimed were some
By crash of the ignited dome.
Staunch stood the walls.   As friars profess
(And not in fraud) the central cell—
Christ's tomb and faith's last citadel—
The flames did tenderly caress,
Nor harm ; while smoking, smouldering beams,
Fallen across, lent livid gleams
To Golgotha.   But none the less
In robed procession of his God
The mitred one the cinders trod ;
Before the calcined altar there
The host he raised ; and hymn and prayer
Went up from ashes.   These, ere chill
Away were brushed ; and trowel shrill
And hod and hammer came in place.
'Tis now some threescore years ago.
   In Lima's first convulsion so,

When shock on shock had left slim trace
Of hundred temples ; and—in mood
Of malice dwelling on the face
Itself has tortured and subdued
To uncomplaint—the cloud pitch-black
Lowered o'er the rubbish ; and the land
Not less than sea, did countermand
Her buried corses—heave them back ;
And flocks and men fled on the track
Which wins the Andes ; then went forth
The prelate with intrepid train
Rolling the anthem 'mid the rain
Of ashes white.   In rocking plain
New boundaries staked they, south and north
For ampler piles.   These stand.   In cheer
The priest reclaimed the quaking sphere.
Hold it he shall, so long as spins
This star of tragedies, this orb of sins.'
    ' That,' Clarel said, ' is not my mind.
Rome's priest forever rule the world ? '
    ' The priest, I said.   Though some be hurled
From anchor, nor a haven find ;
Not less religion's ancient port,
Till the crack of doom, shall be resort
In stress of weather for mankind.
Yea, long as children feel affright
In darkness, men shall fear a God ;
And long as daisies yield delight
Shall see His footprints in the sod.
Is 't ignorance ?   This ignorant state
Science doth but elucidate—
Deepen, enlarge.   But though 'twere made
Demonstrable that God is not—
What then ? it would not change this lot :
The ghost would haunt, nor could be laid.'

Intense he spake, his eyes of blue
Altering, and to eerie hue,
Like Tyrrhene seas when overcast ;
The which Vine noted, nor in joy,
Inferring thence an ocean-waste
Of earnestness without a buoy :
An influence which afterward
Acquaintance led him to discard
Or modify, or not employ.
    Clarel ill-relished.
                      Rolfe, in tone
Half elegiac, thus went on :
' Phylæ, upon thy sacred ground
Osiris' broken tomb is found :
A god how good, whose good proved vain—
In strife with bullying Python slain.
For long the ritual chant or moan
Of pilgrims by that mystic stone
Went up, even much as now ascend
The liturgies of yearning prayer
To one who met a kindred end—
Christ, tombed in turn, and worshipped
    there,'
And pointed.—' Hint you,' here asked Vine,
' In Christ Osiris met decline
Anew ? '—' Nay, nay ; and yet, past doubt,
Strange is that text St. Matthew won
From gray Hosea in sentence : *Out
Of Egypt have I called my son.*'
    Here Clarel spake, and with a stir
Not all assured in eager plight :
' But does not Matthew there refer
Only to the return from flight,
Flight into Egypt ? '—' May be so,'
Said Rolfe ; ' but then Hosea ?—Nay,

We 'll let it pass.'—And fell delay
Of talk ; they mused.—
                             ' To Cicero,'
Rolfe sudden said, ' is a long way
From Matthew ; yet somehow he comes
To mind here—he and his fine tomes,
Which (change the gods) would serve to read
For modern essays.   And indeed
His age was much like ours ; doubt ran,
Faith flagged ; negations which sufficed
Lawyer, priest, statesman, gentleman,
Not yet being popularly prized,
The augurs hence retained some state—
Which served for the illiterate.
Still, the decline so swiftly ran
From stage to stage, that *To Believe*,
Except for slave or artisan,
Seemed heresy.   Even doubts which met
Horror at first, grew obsolete,
And in a decade.   To bereave
Of founded trust in Sire Supreme
Was a vocation.   Sophists throve—
Each weaving his thin thread of dream
Into the shroud for Numa's Jove.
Cæsar his atheism avowed
Before the Senate.   But why crowd
Examples here : the gods were gone.
Tully scarce dreamed they could be won
Back into credence ; less that earth
Ever could know yet mightier birth
Of deity.   He died.   Christ came.
And, in due hour, that impious Rome,
Emerging from vast wreck and shame,
Held the forefront of Christendom.
The inference ? the lesson ?—come :

Let fools count on faith's closing knell—
Time, God, are inexhaustible.—
But what ? so earnest ? ay, again.'
      ' Hard for a fountain to refrain,'
Breathed Vine.   Was that but irony ?
At least no envy in the strain.
Rolfe scarce remarked, or let go by.
      For Clarel—when ye, meeting, scan
In waste the Bagdad caravan,
And solitude puts on the stir,
Clamour, dust, din of Nineveh,
As horsemen, camels, footmen all,
Soldier and merchant, free and thrall,
Pour by in tide processional ;
So to the novice streamed along
Rolfe's filing thoughts, a wildering throng.
Their sway he owned.   And yet how Vine—
Who breathed few words, or gave dumb sign—
Him more allured, suggestive more
Of choicer treasure, rarer store
Reserved, like Kidd's doubloons long sought
Without the wand.
                        The ball of thought
And chain yet dragging, on they strained
Oblique along the upland—slow
And mute, until a point they gained
Where devotees will pause, and know
 A tenderness, may be.   Here then,
While tarry now these pilgrim men,
The interval let be assigned
A niche for image of a novel mind.

XXXII

OF RAMA

That Rama whom the Indian sung—
A god he was, but knew it not ;
Hence vainly puzzled at the wrong
Misplacing him in human lot.
Curtailment of his right he bare
Rather than wrangle ; but no less
Was taunted for his tameness there.
A fugitive without redress,
He never the Holy Spirit grieved,
Nor the divine in him bereaved,
Though what that was he might not guess.

    Live they who, like to Rama, led
Unspotted from the world aside,
Like Rama are discredited—
Like him, in outlawry abide ?
May life and fable so agree ?—
    The innocent if lawless elf,
Ethereal in virginity,
Retains the consciousness of self.
Though black frost nip, though white frost chill,
Nor white frost nor the black may kill
The patient root, the vernal sense
Surviving hard experience
As grass the winter.   Even that curse
Which is the wormwood mixed with gall—
Better dependent on the worse—

Divine upon the animal—
That cannot make such natures fall.

Though yielding easy rein, indeed,
To impulse which the fibres breed,
Nor quarrelling with indolence ;
Shall these the cup of grief dispense
Deliberate to any heart ?
Not craft they know, nor envy's smart.
Theirs be the thoughts that dive and skim,
Theirs the spiced tears that overbrim,
And theirs the dimple and the lightsome whim.

Such natures, and but such, have got
Familiar with strange things that dwell
Repressed in mortals ; and they tell
Of riddles in the prosiest lot.

Mince ye some matter for faith's sake
And heaven's good name ?   'Tis these shall make
Revolt there, and the gloss disclaim.

They con the page kept down with those
Which Adam's secret frame disclose,
And Eve's ; nor dare dissent from truth
Although disreputable, sooth.

The riches in them be a store
Unmerchantable in the ore.
No matter : ' 'Tis an open mine :
Dig ; find ye gold, why, make it thine.
The shrewder knack hast thou, the gift :
Smelt then, and mould, and good go with thy thrift.'

Was ever earth-born wight like this ?
Ay—in the verse, may be, he is.

XXXIII

BY THE STONE

OVER against the Temple here
A monastery unrestored—
Named from Prediction of Our Lord—
Crumbled long since. Outlying near,
Some stones remain, which seats afford :
And one, the fond traditions state,
Is that whereon the Saviour sate
And prophesied, and sad became
To think, what, under sword and flame,
The proud Jerusalem should be,
Then spread before Him sunnily—
Pillars and palms—the white, the green—
Marble enfoliaged, a fair scene ;
But *now*—a vision here conferred
Pale as Pompeii disinterred.

Long Rolfe, on knees his elbows resting
And head enlocked in hands upright,
Sat facing it in steadfast plight
And brooded on that town slow wasting.
' And here,' he said, ' here did He sit—
In leafy covert, say—*Beheld
The city, and wept over it :*
Luke's words, and hard to be excelled,
So just the brief expression there :
Truth's rendering.'—With earnest air,

More he threw out, in kind the same,
The which did Clarel ponder still ;
For though the words might frankness
    claim,
With reverence for site and name ;
No further went they, nor could fill
Faith's measure—scarce her dwindled gill
Now standard. On the plain of Troy
(Mused Clarel) as one might look down
From Gargarus with quiet joy
In verifying Homer's sites,
Yet scarce believe in Venus' crown
And rescues in those Trojan fights
Whereby she saved her supple son ;
So Rolfe regards from these wan heights
Yon walls and slopes to Christians dear.
Much it annoyed him and perplexed :
Than free concession so sincere—
Concession due both site and text—
Dissent itself would less appear
To imply negation.
            But anon
They mark in groups, hard by the gate
Which overlooks Jehoshaphat,
Some Hebrew people of the town.
' Who marvels that outside they come
Since few within have seemly home,'
Said Rolfe ; ' they chat there on the seats,
But seldom gossip in their streets.
Who here may see a busy one ?
Where 's naught to do not much is done.
How live they then ? what bread can be ?
In almost every country known
Rich Israelites these kinsmen own :
The hat goes round the world. But see ! '

Moved by his words, their eyes more reach
Toward that dull group.   Dwarfed in the dream
Of distance sad, penguins they seem
Drawn up on Patagonian beach.

' O city,' Rolfe cried ; ' house on moor,
With shutters burst and blackened door—
Like that thou showest ; and the gales
Still round thee blow the Banshee-wails :
Well might the priest in temple start,
Hearing the voice—" *Woe, we depart !* " '

Clarel gave ear, albeit his glance
Diffident skimmed Vine's countenance,
As mainly here he interest took
In all the fervid speaker said,
Reflected in the mute one's look :
A face indeed quite overlaid
With tremulous meanings, which evade
Or shun regard, nay, hardly brook
Fraternal scanning.
            Rolfe went on :
' The very natives of the town
Methinks would turn from it and flee
But for that curse which is its crown—
That curse which clogs so, poverty.
See them, but see yon cowering men :
The brood—the brood without the hen ! '—

' City, that dost the prophets stone,
How oft against the judgment dread,
How often would I fain have spread
My wings to cover thee, mine own ;
And ye would not !   Had'st thou but known
The things which to thy peace belong ! '

Nehemiah it was, rejoining them—
Gray as the old Jerusalem
Over which how earnestly he hung.
But him the seated audience scan
As he were sole surviving man
Of tribe extinct or world.   The ray
Which lit his features died away ;
He flagged ; and, as some trouble moved,
Apart and aimlessly he roved.

XXXIV

THEY TARRY

' How solitary on the hill
Sitteth the city ; and how still—
How still ! ' From Vine the murmur came—
A cadence, as it were compelled
Even by the picture's silent claim.
That said, again his peace he held,
Biding, as in a misty rain
Some motionless lone fisherman
By mountain brook. But Rolfe : ' Thy word
Is Jeremiah's, and here well heard.
Ay, seer of Anathoth, behold,
Yon object tallies with thy text.
How then ? Stays reason quite unvexed ?
Fulfilment here but falleth cold.
That stable proof which man would fold,
How may it be derived from things
Subject to change and vanishings ?
But let that pass. All now 's revised :
Zion, like Rome, is Niebuhrised.
Yes, doubt attends. Doubt's heavy hand
Is set against us ; and his brand
Still warreth for his natural lord—
King Common-Place—whose rule abhorred
Yearly extends in vulgar sway,
Absorbs Atlantis and Cathay ;
Ay, reaches toward Diana's moon,
Affirming it a clinkered blot,
Deriding pale Endymion.

Since thus he aims to level all,
The Milky Way he 'll yet allot
For Appian to his Capital.
Then tell, tell then, what charm may save
Thy marvel, Palestine, from grave
Whereto winds many a bier and pall
Of old Illusion ?   What for earth ?
Ah, change irreverent—at odds
With goodly customs, gracious gods ;
New things elate so thrust their birth
Up through dejection of the old,
As through dead sheaths ; is here foretold
The consummation of the past,
And garish dawning of a day
Whose noon not saints desire to stay—
And hardly I ?   Who brake love's fast
With Christ—with what strange lords may
    sup ?
The reserves of time seem marching up.
But, nay : what novel thing may be,
No germ being new ?   By Fate's decree
Have not earth's vitals heaved in change
Repeated ? some wild element
Or action been evolved ? the range
Of surface split ? the deeps unpent ?
Continents in God's cauldrons cast ?
And this without effecting so
The neutralising of the past,
Whose rudiments persistent flow,
From age to age transmitting, own,
The evil with the good—the taint
Deplored in Solomon's complaint.
Fate's pot of ointment !   Wilt have done,
Lord of the fly, god of the grub ?
Need'st foul all sweets, thou Beelzebub ? '

He ended.—To evade or lay
Deductions hard for tender clay,
Clarel recalled each prior word
Of Rolfe which scarcely kept accord,
As seemed, with much dropped latterly.
For Vine, he twitched from ground a weed,
Apart then picked it, seed by seed.

　　Ere long they rise, and climbing greet
A thing pre-eminent in seat,
Whose legend still can touch the heart :
It prompted one there to impart
A chapter of the Middle Age—
Which next to give.　But let the page
The narrator's rambling way forget,
And make to run in even flow
His interrupted tale.　And let
Description brief the site foreshow.

XXXV

In spot revered by myriad men,
Whence, as alleged, Immanuel rose
Into the heaven—receptive then—
A little plastered tower is set,
Pale in the light that Syria knows,
Upon the peak of Olivet.
'Tis modern—a replacement, note,
For ample pile of years remote,
Nor yet ill suits in dwindled bound
Man's faith retrenched.   'Twas Hakeem's deed,
Mad Caliph (founder still of creed
Long held by tribes not unrenowned)
Who erst the pastoral height discrowned
Of Helena's church.   Woe for the dome,
And many a goodly temple more,
Which hither lured from Christendom
The childlike pilgrim throngs of yore.
'Twas of that church, so brave erewhile—
Blest landmark on the Olive Height—
Which Arculf told of in the isle
Iona.   Shipwrecked there in sight,
The palmer dragged they from the foam,
The Culdees of the abbey fair—
Him shelter yielding and a home.
In guerdon for which love and care
Received in Saint Columba's pile,
With travel-talk he did beguile
Their eve of Yule.

                The tempest beat ;
It shook the abbey's founded seat,
Rattling the crucifix on wall ;
And thrice was heard the clattering fall
Of gable-tiles.　But host and guest,
Abbot and palmer, took their rest
Inside monastic ingle tall.
What unto them were those lashed seas ?
Or Patmos or the Hebrides,
The isles were God's.
                It was the time
The church in Jewry dwelt at ease
Tho' under Arabs—Omar's prime—
Penultimate of pristine zeal,
While yet throughout faith's commonweal
The tidings had not died away—
Not yet had died into dismay
Of dead, dead echoes that recede :
Glad tidings of great joy indeed,
Thrilled to the shepherds on the sward—
' *Behold, to you is born this day*
A Saviour, which is Christ the Lord ' ;
While yet in chapel, altar, shrine,
The mica in the marble new
Glistened like spangles of the dew.
One minster then was Palestine,
All monumental.
                Arculf first
The wonders of the tomb rehearsed,
And Golgotha ;　then told of trees,
Olives, which in the twilight breeze
Sighed plaintive by the convent's lee—
The convent in Gethsemane—
Perished long since.　Then :　' On the
      hill—

In site revealed thro' Jesu's grace '—
(Hereat both cross themselves apace)
' A great round church with goodly skill
Is nobly built ; and fragrant blows
Morning thro' triple porticoes.
But over that blest place where meet
The last prints of the Wounded Feet,
The roof is open to the sky ;
'Tis there the sparrows love to fly.
Upon Ascension Day—at end
Of mass—winds, vocal winds descend
Among the worshippers.'   Amain
The abbot signs the cross again ;
And Arculf on : ' And all that night
The mountain temple's western flank—
The same which fronts Moriah's height—
In memory of the Apostles' light
Shows twelve dyed fires in oriels twelve.
Thither, from towers on Kedron's bank
And where the slope and terrace shelve,
The gathered townsfolk gaze afar ;
And those twelve flowers of flame suffuse
Their faces with reflected hues
Of violet, gold, and cinnabar.
Much so from Naples (in our sail
We touched there, shipping jar and bale)
I saw Vesuvius' plume of fire
Redden the bay, tinge mast and spire.
But on Ascension Eve, 'tis then
A light shows—kindled not by men.
Look,' pointing to the hearth ; ' dost see
How these dun embers here by me,
Lambent are licked by flaky flame ?
Olivet gleams then much the same—
Caressed, curled over, yea, encurled

By fleecy fires which typic be :
O Lamb of God, O Light o' the World ! '
   In fear, and yet a fear divine,
Once more the Culdee made the sign ;
Then fervid snatched the palmer's hand—
Clung to it like a very child
Thrilled by some wondrous story wild
Of elf or fay, nor could command
His eyes to quit their gaze at him—
Him who had seen it. But how grim
The Pictish storm-king sang refrain,
Scoffing about those gables high
Over Arculf and good Adamnan.

   The abbot and the palmer rest :
The legends follow them and die—
Those legends which, be it confessed,
Did nearer bring to them the sky—
Did nearer woo it to their hope
Of all that seers and saints avow—
Than Galileo's telescope
Can bid it unto prosing Science now.

XXXVI

THE TOWER

THE tower they win.   Some Greeks at hand,
Pilgrims, in silence view the land.
One family group in listless tone
Are just in act of faring down.
All leave at last.   And these remain
As by a hearthstone on the plain
When roof is gone.   But can they shame
To tell the evasive thought within ?
Does intellect assert a claim
Against the heart, her yielding kin ?
  But he, the wanderer, the while—
See him ; and what may so beguile ?
Images he the ascending Lord
Pale as the moon which dawn may meet,
Convoyed by a serene accord
And swoon of faces young and sweet—
Mid chaplets, stars,·and halcyon wings,
And many ministering things ?
  As him they mark enkindled so,
What inklings, negatives, they know !
But leaving him in silence due,
They enter there, the print to view—
Affirmed of Christ—the parting foot :
They mark it, nor a question moot ;
Next climb the stair and win the roof ;
Thence on Jerusalem look down,
And Kedron cringing by the town,

143

Whose stony lanes map-like were shown.
    ' Is yon the city Dis aloof ? '
Said Rolfe ; ' nay, liker 'tis some print,
Old blurred, bewrinkled mezzotint.
And distant, look, what lifeless hills !
Dead long for them the hymn of rills
And birds.   Nor trees nor ferns they know ;
Nor lichen there hath leave to grow
In baleful glens which blacked the blood
O' the son of Kish.'
                    Far peep they gain
Of waters which in cauldron brood,
Sunk mid the mounts of leaden bane :
The Sodom Wave, or Putrid Sea,
Or Sea of Salt, or Cities Five,
Or Lot's, or Death's, Asphaltite,
Or Asafœtida ; all these
Being names indeed with which they gyve
That site of foul iniquities
Abhorred.
           With wordless look intent,
As if the scene confirmed some thought
Which in heart's lonelier hour was lent,
Vine stood at gaze.   The rest were wrought
According unto kind.   The Mount
Of Olives, and, in distance there
The charnel wave—who may recount ?
Hope's hill descries the pit Despair :
Flitted the thought ; they nothing said ;
And down they drew.   As ground they tread,
Nehemiah met them : ' Pleaseth ye,
Fair stroll awaits ; if all agree,
Over the hill let us go on—
Bethany is a pleasant town,
I 'll lead, for well the way I know.'

He gazed expectant : Would they go ?
Before that simpleness so true
Vine showed embarrassed (Clarel too)
Yet thanked him with a grateful look
Benign ; and Rolfe the import took,
And whispered him in softened key,
' Some other day.'
　　　　　　　And might it be
Such influence their spirits knew
From all the tower had given to view,
Untuned they felt for Bethany ?

XXXVII

A SKETCH

NOT knowing them in very heart
Nor why to join him they were loth,
He, disappointed, moved apart,
With sad pace creeping, dull, as doth
Along the bough the nerveless sloth.

For ease upon the ground they sit ;
And Rolfe, with eye still following
Where Nehemiah slow-footed it,
Asked Clarel : ' Know you anything
Of this man's prior life at all ? '
' Nothing,' said Clarel.—' I recall,'
Said Rolfe, ' a mariner like him.'
' A mariner ? '—' Yes ; one whom grim
Disaster made as meek as he
There plodding.'   Vine here showed the zest
Of a deep human interest :
' We crave of you his history ' :
     And Rolfe began : ' Scarce would I tell
Of what this mariner befell—
So much is it with cloud o'ercast—
Were he not now gone home at last
Into the green land of the dead,
Where he encamps and peace is shed.
Hardy he was, sanguine and bold,
The master of a ship.   His mind
In night-watch frequent he unrolled—
As seamen sometimes are inclined—

On serious topics, to his mate,
A man to creed austere resigned.
The master ever spurned at fate,
Calvin's or Zeno's.   Always still
Man-like he stood by man's free will
And power to effect each thing he would,
Did reason but pronounce it good.
The subaltern held in humble way
That still Heaven's overrulings sway
Will and event.
      ' On waters far,
Where map-man never made survey,
Gliding along in easy plight,
The strong one brake the lull of night
Emphatic in his wilful war—
But staggered, for there came a jar
With fell arrest to keel and speech :
A hidden rock.   The pound—the grind—
Collapsing sails o'er deck declined—
Sleek billows curling in the breach,
And nature with her neutral mind.
A wreck.   'Twas in the former days,
Those waters then obscure ; a maze ;
The isles were dreaded—every chain ;
Better to brave the immense of sea,
And venture for the Spanish Main,
Beating and rowing against the trades,
Than float to valleys 'neath the lee,
Nor far removed, and palmy shades.
So deemed he, strongly erring there.
To boats they take ; the weather fair—
Never the sky a cloudlet knew ;
A temperate wind unvarying blew
Week after week ; yet came despair ;
The bread tho' doled, and water stored

Ran low and lower—ceased. They burn—
They agonise till crime abhorred
Lawful might be. O trade-wind, turn !
      ' Well may some items sleep unrolled—
Never by the one survivor told.
Him they picked up, where, cuddled down,
They saw the jacketed skeleton,
Lone in the only boat that lived—
His signal frittered to a shred.
      ' " Strong need'st thou be," the rescuers said,
" Who hast such trial sole survived."
" I *willed* it," gasped he. And the man,
Renewed ashore, pushed off again.
How bravely sailed the pennoned ship
Bound outward on her sealing trip
Antarctic. Yes ; but who returns
Too soon, regaining port by land
Who left it by the bay ? What spurns
Were his that so could countermand ?
Nor mutineer, nor rock, nor gale
Nor leak had foiled him. No ; a whale
Of purpose aiming, stove the bow :
They foundered. To the master now
Owners and neighbours all impute
An inauspiciousness. His wife—
Gentle, but unheroic—she,
Poor thing, at heart knew bitter strife
Between her love and her simplicity :
A Jonah is he ?—And men bruit
The story. None will give him place
In a third venture. Came the day
Dire need constrained the man to pace
A night patrolman on the quay
Watching the bales till morning hour
Through fair and foul. Never he smiled ;

Call him, and he would come ; not sour
In spirit, but meek and reconciled ;
Patient he was, he none withstood ;
Oft on some secret thing would brood.
He ate what came, though but a crust ;
In Calvin's creed he put his trust ;
Praised heaven, and said that God was good,
And his calamity but just.
So Sylvio Pellico from cell-door
Forth tottering, after dungeoned years,
Crippled and bleached, and dead his peers :
" Grateful, I thank the Emperor." '

There ceasing, after pause Rolfe drew
Regard to Nehemiah in view :
' Look, the changed master, roams he there ?
I mean, is such the guise, the air ? '
The speaker sat between mute Vine
And Clarel.   From the mystic sea
Laocoon's serpent, sleek and fine,
In loop on loop seemed here to twine
His clammy coils about the three.
Then unto them the wannish man
Draws nigh ; but absently they scan ;
A phantom seems he, and from zone
Where naught is real tho' the winds aye moan.

XXXVIII

THE SPARROW

AFTER the hint by Rolfe bestowed,
Redoubled import, one may ween,
Had Nehemiah's submissive mien
For Clarel.   Nay, his poor abode—
And thither now the twain repair—
A new significance might bear.

  Thin grasses, such as sprout in sand,
Clarel observes in crannies old
Along the cornice.   Not his hand
The mower fills with such, nor arms
Of him that binds the sheaf, enfold.
Now mid the quiet which becharms
That mural wilderness remote,
Querulous came the little note
Of bird familiar—one of them
So numerous in Jerusalem,
Still snared for market, it is told,
And two were for a farthing sold—
The sparrow.   But this single one
Plaining upon a terrace nigh,
Was like the Psalmist's making moan
For loss of mate—forsaken quite,
Which on the house-top doth alight
And watches, and her lonely cry
No answer gets.—In sunny height
Like dotting bees against the sky
What twitterers o'er the Temple fly !

But now the arch and stair they gain,
And in the chamber sit the twain.
Clarel in previous time secure,
From Nehemiah had sought to lure
Some mention of his life, but failed.
Rolfe's hintful story so prevailed,
Anew he thought to venture it.
But while in so much else aside
Subject to senile lapse of tide,
In this hid matter of his past
The saint evinced a guardful wit ;
His waning energies seemed massed
Here, and but here, to keep the door.
At present his reserve of brow
Reproach in such sort did avow,
That Clarel never pressed him more.
Nay, fearing lest he trespass might
Even in tarrying longer now,
He parted.   As he slow withdrew,
Well pleased he noted in review
The hermitage improved in plight.
　　Some one had done a friendly thing :
Who ?   Small was Clarel's wondering.

XXXIX

CLAREL AND RUTH

In northern clime how tender show
The meads beneath heaven's humid Bow
When showers draw off and dewdrops cling
To sunset's skirt, and robins sing
Though night be near.   So did the light
Of love redeem in Ruth the trace
Of grief, though scarce might it efface.
　　From wider rambles which excite
The thought, or study's lone repose,
Daily did Clarel win the close.
With interest feminine and true
The matron watched that love which grew ;
She hailed it, since a hope was there
Made brighter for the grief's degree :
How shines the gull ye watch in air
White, white against the cloud at sea.
　　Clarel, bereft while still but young,
Mother or sister had not known ;
To him now first in life was shown,
In Agar's frank demeanour kind,
What charm to woman may belong
When by a natural bent inclined
To goodness in domestic play :
On earth no better thing than this—
It canonises very clay :
Madonna, hence thy worship is.

But Ruth : since Love had signed with Fate
The bond, and the first kiss had sealed,
Both for her own and Agar's state
Much of her exile-grief seemed healed :
New vistas opened ; and if still
Forebodings might not be forgot
As to her sire's eventual lot,
Yet hope, which is of youth, could thrill.
That frame to foster and defend,
Clarel, when in her presence, strove
The unrest to hide which still could blend
With all the endearings of their love.
Ruth part divined the lurking care,
But more the curb, and motive too :
It made him but love's richer heir ;
So much the more attachment grew.
She could not think but all would prove
Subject in end to mighty Love.
That cloud which in the present reigned,
By flushful hope's aurora stained,
At times redeemed itself in hues
Of shell, and humming-bird, and flower.
Could Heaven two loyal hearts abuse ?
The death-moth, let him keep his bower.

XL

Ere twilight and the shadow fall
On Zion hill without the wall
In place where Latins set the bier
Borne from the gate—who lingers here,
Where, typing faith exempt from loss,
By sodless mound is seen a cross ?
Clarel it is, at Celio's grave.
For him, the pale one, ere yet cold,
Assiduous to win and save,
The friars had claimed as of their fold ;
Lit by the light of ritual wicks,
Had held to unprotesting lips
In mistimed zeal the crucifix ;
And last, among the fellowships
Of Rome's legitimate dead, laid one
Not saved through faith, nor Papal Rome's true
    son.
Life's flickering hour they made command
Faith's candle in Doubt's dying hand.
So some, who other forms did hold,
Rumoured, or criticised, or told
The tale.
        Not this did Clarel win
To visit the hermit of the mound.
Nay, but he felt the appeal begin—
The poor petition from the ground :
Remember me ! for all life's din
Let not my memory be drowned.

154

And thought was Clarel's even for one
Of tribe not his—to him unknown
Through vocal word or vital cheer :
A stranger, but less strange made here,
Less distant.   Whom life held apart—
Life, whose cross-purposes make shy—
Death yields without reserve of heart
To meditation.
                    With a sigh
Turning, he slow pursued the steep
Until he won that levelled spot,
Terraced and elevated plot
Over Gihon, where yet others keep
Death's tryst—afar from kindred lie :
Protestants, which in Salem die.
        There, fixed before a founded stone
With Bible mottoes part bestrown,
Stood one communing with the bier.
'Twas Rolfe.   ' Him, him I knew,' said he,
Down pointing ; ' but 'twas far from here—
How far from here ! '   A pause.   ' But see,
Job's text in wreath, what trust it giveth ;
" I KNOW THAT MY REDEEMER LIVETH."
Poor Ethelward !   Thou didst but grope ;
I knew thee, and thou hadst small hope.
But if at this spent man's death-bed
Some kind soul kneeled and chapter read—
Ah, own ! to moderns death is drear,
So drear : we die, we make no sign,
We acquiesce in any cheer—
No rite we seek, no rite decline.
Is 't nonchalance of languid sense,
Or the last, last indifference ?
With some, no doubt, 'tis peace within ;
In others, may be, care for kin :

Exemplary thro' life, as well
Dying they 'd be so, nor repel.'
   He let his eyes half-absent move
About the mound : ' One's thoughts will rove :
This minds me that in like content,
Other forms were kept without dissent
By one who hardly owned their spell.
He, in fulfilment of pledged work,
Among Turks having passed for Turk,
Sickened among them.   On death-bed
Silent he heard the Koran read :
They shrilled the Islam wail for him,
They shawled him in his burial trim ;
And now, on brinks of Egypt's waste,
Where the buried Sultans' chapels rise,
Consistently toward Mecca faced,
The blameless simulator lies :
The turbaned Swiss, Sheik Ibrahim—
Burckhardt.—But home the sparrow flees.
Come, move we ere the gate they quit,
And we be shut out here with these
Who never shall re-enter it.'

XLI

ON THE WALL

THEY parted in the port.   Near by,
Long stone stairs win the battlement
Of wall, aerial gallery ;
And thither now the student bent
To muse abroad.

              The sun's last rays
Shed round a nearing train the haze
Of mote and speck.   Advanced in view
And claiming chief regard, came two
Dismounted, barefoot ; one in dress
Expressive of deep humbleness
Of spirit, scarce of social state—
His lineaments rebutted that,
Tho' all was overcast with pain—
The visage of a doom-struck man
Not idly seeking holy ground.
Behind, his furnished horse did bound
Checked by a groom in livery fair.
The master paced in act of prayer
Absorbed—went praying thro' the gate.
The attentive student, struck thereat,
The wall crossed—from the inner arch
Viewed him emerging, while in starch
Of prelate robes, some waiting Greeks
Received him, kissed him on both cheeks,
Showing that specialising love
And deference grave, how far above
What Lazarus in grief may get ;

Nor less sincere those priests were yet.
    Second in the dismounted list
Was one, a laic votarist,
The cross and chaplet by his side,
Sharing the peace of eventide
In frame devout. A Latin he,
But not, as seemed, of high degree.
Such public reverence profound
In crossing Salem's sacred bound
Is not so common, in late day,
But that the people by the way
In silent-viewing eyes confessed
The spectacle had interest.
    Nazarene Hebrews twain rode next,
By one of the escort slyly vexed.
In litter borne by steady mules
A Russian lady parts the screen ;
A rider, as the gate is seen,
Dismounts, and her alighting rules—
Her husband. Checkered following there,
Like envoys from all Adam's race,
Mixed men of various nations pace,
Such as in crowded steamer come
And disembark at Jaffa's stair.
    Mute mid the buzz of chat and prayer,
Plain-clad where others sport the plume,
What countrymen are yonder three ?
The critic-coolness in their eyes
Disclaims emotion's shallow sea ;
Or misapply they precept wise,
Nil admirari ? Or, may be,
Rationalists these riders are,
Men self-sufficing, insular.
Nor less they show in grave degree
Tolerance for each poor votary.

Now when the last rays slanting fall,
The last new-comer enters in :
The gate shuts after with a din.
Tarries the student on the wall.
Dubieties of recent date—
Scenes, words, events—he thinks of all.
As, when the autumn sweeps the down,
And gray skies tell of summer gone,
The swallow hovers by the strait—
Impending on the passage long ;
Upon a brink and poise he hung.
The bird in end must needs migrate
Over the sea : shall Clarel too
Launch o'er *his* gulf, e'en Doubt, and woo
Remote conclusions ?
                     Unresigned,
He sought the inn, and tried to read
The Fathers with a filial mind.
In vain ; heart wandered or repined.
The Evangelists may serve his need :
Deep as he felt the beauty sway,
Estrangement there he could but heed,
Both time and tone so far away
From him the modern. Not to dwell,
Rising he walked the floor, then stood
Irresolute. His eye here fell
Upon the blank wall of the cell,
The wall before him, and he viewed
A place where the last coat of lime—
White flakes whereof lay dropped below—
Thin scaling off, laid open so
Upon the prior coat a rhyme
Pale pencilled. In one's nervous trance
Things near will distant things recall,
And common ones suggest romance :

He thought of her built up in wall,
Cristina of Coll'alto ; yes,
The verse here breaking from recess—
Tho' immaterial, but a thought
In some sojourning traveller wrought—
Scribbled, overlaid, again revealed—
Seemed like a tragic fact unsealed :
So much can mood possess a man.
        He read : obscurely thus it ran :—

  ' For me who never loved the stride,
Triumph and taunt that shame the winning
        side—
Toward Him over whom, in expectation's glow,
Elate the advance of rabble-banners gleam—
Turned from a world that dare renounce Him so,
My unweaned thoughts in steadfast trade-wind
        stream,
If Atheists and Vitriolists of doom
Faith's gathering night with rockets red illume—
So much the more in pathos I adore
The low lamps flickering in Syria's Tomb.'—

  ' What strain is this ?—But, here, in blur,
" After return from Sepulchre :
B. L." '—On the ensuing day
He plied the host with question free :
Who answered him, ' A pilgrim—nay,
How to remember !   English, though—
A fair young Englishman.   But stay ' :
And after absence brief he slow
With volumes came in hand : ' These, look—
He left behind by chance.'—One book,
With portrait of a mitred man,
Treated of High Church Anglican,

Confession, fast, saint-day—deplored
That rubric old was not restored.
But under *Finis* there was writ
A comment that made grief of it.
    The second work hath other cheer—
Started from Strauss, disdained Renan—
By striding paces up to Pan ;
Nor rested, but the goat-god here
Capped with the red cap in the twist
Of Proudhon and the Communist.
But random jottings in the marge
Disclosed some reader of the text
Whose fervid comments did discharge
More dole than e'en dissent.   Annexed,
In either book was pencilled small :
' B. L. : Oxford : St. Mary's Hall.'

    Such proved these volumes—such, as scanned
By Clarel, wishful to command
Some hint that might supply a clue
Better enabling to construe
The lines their owner left on wall.

XLII

TIDINGS

Some of the strangers late arrived
Tarried with Abdon at the inn ;
And, ere long, having viewed the town
Would travel further, and pass on
To Siddim, and the Dead Sea win
And Saba.   And would Clarel go ?
'Twas but for days.   They would return
By Bethlehem, and there sojourn
Awhile, regaining Zion so.
But Clarel undetermined stood,
And kept his vacillating mood,
Though learning, as it happed, that Vine
And Rolfe would join the journeying band.
    Loath was he here to disentwine
Himself from Ruth.   Nor less Lot's land,
And sea, and Judah's utmost drought
Fain would he view, and mark their tone :
And prove if, unredeemed by John,
John's wilderness augmented doubt.
As chanced, while wavering in mind,
And threading a hushed lane or wynd
Quick warning shout he heard behind
And clattering hoofs.   He hugged the wall,
Then turned ;   in that brief interval
The dust came on him, powdery light,
From one who like a javelin flew
Spectral with dust, and all his plight
Charged with the desert and its hue ;

A courier, and he bent his flight
(As Clarel afterward recalled)
Whither lay Agar's close inwalled.
　　The clank of arms, the clink of shoe,
The cry admonitory too,
Smote him, and yet he scarce knew why ;
But when, some hours having flitted by,
Nearing the precincts of the Jew
His host, he did Nehemiah see
Waiting in arch, and with a look
Which some announcement's shadow took,
His heart stood still—Fate's herald, he ?
　　' What is it ? what ? '—The saint delayed.—
' Ruth ? '—' Nathan ' ; and the news conveyed.
The threat, oft hurled, as oft reviled
By one too proud to give it heed,
The menace of stern foemen wild,
No menace now was, but a deed :
Burned was the roof on Sharon's plain ;
And timbers charred showed clotted stain :
But, spirited away, each corse
Unsepulchred remained, or worse.

　　Ah, Ruth—woe, Agar ! Ill breeds ill ;
The widow with no future free,
Without resource perhaps, or skill
To steer upon grief's misty sea.
　　To grieve with them and lend his aid,
Straight to the house see Clarel fare,
The house of mourning—sadder made
For that the mourned one lay not there—
But found it barred. He, waiting so,
Doubtful to knock or call them—lo,
The Rabbi issues, while behind
The door shuts to. The meeting eyes

Reciprocate a quick surprise,
Then alter ; and the secret mind
The Rabbi bears to Clarel shows
In dark superior look he throws :
Censorious consciousness of power :
Death—and it is the Levite's hour.
No word he speaks, but turns and goes.
  The student lingered.   He was told
By one without, a neighbour old,
That never Jewish modes relent :
Sealed long would be the tenement
To all but Hebrews—of which race
Kneeled comforters by sorrow's side.
So both were cared for.   Clogged in pace
He turned away.   How pass the tide
Of Ruth's seclusion ?   Might he gain
Relief from dull inaction's pain ?
Yes, join he would those pilgrims now
Which on the morrow would depart
For Siddim, by way of Jericho.
  But first of all, he letters sent,
Brief, yet dictated by the heart—
Announced his plan's constrained intent
Reluctant ; and consigned a ring
For pledge of love and Ruth's remembering.

XLIII

BUT what !—nay, nay : without adieu
Of vital word, dear presence true,
Part shall I ?—break away from love ?
But think : the circumstances move,
And warrant it. Shouldst thou abide,
Cut off yet wert thou from her side
For time : tho' she be sore distressed,
Herself would whisper : ' Go—'tis best.'

    Unstable ! It was in a street,
Half vault, where few or none do greet,
He paced. Anon, encaved in wall
A fount arrests him, sculpture wrought
After a Saracen design—
Ruinous now and arid all
Save dusty weeds which trail or twine.
While lingering in way that brought
The memory of the Golden Bowl
And Pitcher broken, music rose—
Young voices ; a procession shows :
A litter rich, with flowery wreath,
Singers and censers, and a veil.
She comes, the bride ; but, ah, how pale :
Her groom that Blue-Beard, cruel Death,
Wedding his millionth maid to-day ;
She, stretched on that Armenian bier,
Leaves home and each familiar way—
Quits all for him. Nearer, more near—

165

Till now the ineffectual flame
Of burning tapers borne he saw :
The westering sun puts these to shame.

But, hark : responsive marching choirs,
Robed men and boys, in rhythmic law
A contest undetermined keep :
Ay, as the bass in dolings deep
The serious, solemn thought inspires—
In unconcern of rallying sort
The urchin-treble shrills retort ;
But, true to part imposed, again
The beards dirge out.   And so they wind
Till thro' the city gate the train
Files forth to sepulchre.
                              Behind
Left in his hermitage of mind,
What troubles Clarel ?   See him there
As if admonishment in air
He heard.   Can love be fearful so ?
Jealous of fate ? the future ? all
Reverse—mischance ? nay, even the pall
And pit ?—No, I 'll not leave her : no,
'Tis fixed ; I waver now no more.—
        But yet again he thought it o'er,
And self-rebukeful, and with mock :
Thou superstitious doubter—own,
Biers need be borne ; why such a shock
When passes this Armenian one ?
The word 's dispatched, and wouldst recall ?
'Tis but for fleeting interval.

XLIV

THE START

THE twilight and the starlight pass,
And breaks the morn of Candlemas.
      The pilgrims muster ; and they win
A common terrace of the inn,
Which, lifted on Mount Acra's cope,
Looks off upon the town aslope
In gray of dawn.   They hear the din
Of mongrel Arabs—the loud coil
And uproar of high words they wage
Harnessing for the pilgrimage.
'Tis special—marks the Orient life,
Which, roused from indolence to toil,
Indignant starts, enkindling strife.
Tho' spite the fray no harm they share,
How fired they seem by burning wrong ;
And small the need for strenuous care,
And languor yet shall laze it long.
      Wonted to man and used to fate
A pearl-gray ass there stands sedate
While being saddled by a clown
And buffeted.   Of her anon.

      Clarel regards ; then turns his eye
Away from all, beyond the town,
Where pale against the tremulous sky
Olivet shows in morning shy ;
Then on the court again looks down.

The mountain mild, the wrangling crew—
In contrast, why should these indue
With vague unrest, and swell the sigh ?
Add to the burden ? tease the sense
With unconfirmed significance ?
 To horse.   And, passing one by one
Their host the Black Jew by the gate,
His grave salute they take, nor shun
His formal God-speed.   One, elate
In air Auroral, June of life,
With quick and gay response is rife.
But he, the Israelite alone,
'Tis he reflects Jehovah's town ;
Experienced he, the vain elation gone ;
While flit athwart his furrowed face
Glimpses of that ambiguous thought
Which in some aged men ye trace
When Venture, Youth and Bloom go by ;
Scarce cynicism, though 'tis wrought
Not all of pity, since it scants the sigh.

 They part.   Farewell to Zion's seat.
Ere yet anew her place they greet,
In heart what hap may Clarel prove ?
Brief term of days, but a profound remove.

END OF PART I

PART II
THE WILDERNESS

I

THE CAVALCADE

ADOWN the Dolorosa Lane
The mounted pilgrims file in train
Whose clatter jars each open space ;
Then, muffled in, shares change apace
As, striking sparks in vaulted street,
Clink, as in cave, the horses' feet.
    Not from brave Chaucer's Tabard Inn
They pictured wend ; scarce shall they win
Fair Kent, and Canterbury ken ;
Nor franklin, squire, nor morris dance
Of wit and story good as then :
Another age, and other men,
And life an unfulfilled romance.

    First went the turban—guide and guard
In escort armed and desert trim ;
The pilgrims next : whom now to limn.
One there the light rein slackly drew,
And skimming glanced, dejected never—
While yet the pilgrimage was new—
On sights ungladsome howsoever.
Cordial he turned his aspect clear
On all that passed ; man, yea, and brute
Enheartening by a blithe salute,
Chirrup, or pat, in random cheer.
This pleasantness, which might endear,
Suffused was with a prosperous look
That bordered vanity, but took

Fair colour as from ruddy heart.
  A priest he was—though but in part ;
For as the Templar old combined
The cavalier and monk in one ;
In Derwent likewise might you find
The secular and cleric tone.
Imported or domestic mode,
Thought's last adopted style he showed ;
Abreast kept with the age, the year,
And each bright optimistic mind,
Nor lagged with Solomon in rear,
And Job, the furthermost behind—
Brisk marching in time's drum-corps van
Abreast with whistling Jonathan.
Tho' English, with an English home,
His spirits through Creole cross derived
The light and effervescent foam ;
And youth in years mature survived.
At saddle-bow a book was laid
Convenient—tinted in the page
Which did urbanely disengage
Sadness and doubt from all things sad
And dubious deemed.   Confirmed he read :
A priest o' the club—a taking man,
And rather more than Lutheran.
A cloth cape, light in air afloat,
And easy set of cleric coat,
Seemed emblems of that facile wit,
Which suits the age—a happy fit.

  Behind this good man's stirrups rode
A solid stolid Elder, shod
With formidable boots.   He went
Like Talus in a foundry cast ;
Furrowed his face, with wrinkles massed.

He claimed no indirect descent
From Grampian kirk and covenant.
   But recent sallying from home,
Late he assigned three days to Rome.
He saw the host go by. The crowd,
Made up from many a tribe and place
Of Christendom, kept seemly face :
Took off the hat, or kneeled, or bowed ;
But he the helm rammed down apace :
Discourteous to the host, agree,
Tho' to a parting soul it went ;
Nor deemed that, were it mummery,
'Twas pathos too. This hard dissent—
Transferred to Salem in remove—
Led him to carp, and try disprove
Legend and site by square and line :
Aside time's violet mist he 'd shove—
Quite disenchant the Land Divine.
So fierce he hurled zeal's javelin home,
It drove beyond the mark—pierced Rome,
And plunged beyond, thro' enemy
To friend. Scarce natural piety
Might live, abiding such a doom.
Traditions beautiful and old
Which with maternal arms enfold
Millions, else orphaned and made poor,
No plea could lure him to endure.
Concerned, meek Christian ill might bear
To mark this worthy brother rash,
Deeming he served religion there,
Work up the fag-end of Voltaire,
And help along faith's final crash—
If that impend.
           His fingers pressed
A ferrule of blackthorn : he bore

A pruning-knife in belt ; in vest
A measuring-tape wound round a core ;
And field-glass slung athwart the chest ;
While peeped from holsters old and brown,
Horse-pistols—and they were his own.

A hale one followed, good to see,
English and Greek in pedigree ;
Of middle-age ; a ripe gallant,
A banker of the rich Levant ;
In florid opulence preserved
Like peach in syrup. Ne'er he swerved
From morning bath, and dinner boon,
And velvet nap in afternoon,
And lounge in garden with cigar.
His home was Thessalonica,
Which views Olympus. But, may be,
Little he weened of Jove and gods
In synod mid those brave abodes ;
Nor, haply, read or weighed Paul's plea
Addressed from Athens o'er the sea
Unto the Thessalonians old :
His bonds he scanned, and weighed his gold.
   Parisian was his garb, and gay.
Upon his saddle-pommel lay
A rich Angora rug, for shawl
Or pillow, just as need might fall ;
Not the Brazilian leopard's hair
Or toucan's plume may show more fair ;
Yet, serving light convenience mere,
Proved but his heedless affluent cheer.
   Chief exercise this sleek one took
Was toying with a tissue book
At intervals, and leaf by leaf
Gently reducing it. In brief,

With tempered yet Capuan zest,
Of cigarettes he smoked the best.
This wight did Lady Fortune love :
Day followed day in treasure-trove.
Nor only so, but he did run
In unmistrustful reveries bright
Beyond his own career to one
Who should continue it in light
Of lineal good times.
                           High walled,
An Eden owned he nigh his town,
Which locked in leafy emerald
A frescoed lodge.   There Nubians armed,
Tall eunuchs virtuous in zeal,
In shining robes, with glittering steel,
Patrolled about his daughter charmed,
Inmost inclosed in nest of bowers,
By gorgons served, the dread she-powers,
Duennas : maiden more than fair :
How fairer in his rich conceit—
An Argive face, and English hair
Sunny as May in morning sweet :
A damsel for Apollo meet ;
And yet a mortal's destined bride—
Bespoken, yes, affianced late
To one who by the senior's side
Rode rakishly deliberate—
A sprig of Smyrna, Glaucon he.
His father (such ere long to be)
Well loved him, nor that sole he felt
That fortune here had kindly dealt
Another court-card into hand—
The youth with gold at free command ;—
No, but he also liked his clan,
His kinsmen, and his happy way ;

And over wine would pleased repay
His parasites : Well may ye say
The boy 's the bravest gentleman !—
 From Beyrout late had come the pair
To further schemes of finance hid,
And for a pasha's favour bid
And grave connivance. That affair
Yet lingered. So, dull time to kill,
They wandered, anywhere, at will.
Scarce through self-knowledge or self-love
They ventured Judah's wilds to rove,
As time, ere long, and place, may prove.

 Came next in file three sumpter mules
With all things needful for the tent,
And panniers which the Greek o'errules ;
For there, with store of nourishment,
Rosoglio pink and wine of gold
Slumbered as in the smugglers' hold.

 Viewing those Levantines in way
Of the snared lion, which from grate
Marks the light throngs on holiday,
Nor e'er relaxes in his state
Austerely sad ; rode one whose air
Revealed—but, for the nonce, forbear.
Mortmain his name, or so in whim
Some moral wit had christened him.

 Upon that creature men traduce
For patience under their abuse ;
For whose requital there 's assigned
No heaven ; that thing of dreamful kind—
The ass—elected for the ease,
Good Nehemiah followed these ;

His Bible under arm, and leaves
Of tracts still fluttering in sheaves.
In pure goodwill he bent his view
To right and left. The ass, pearl-gray,
Matched well the rider's garb in hue,
And sorted with the ashy way ;
Upon her shoulders' jointed play
The white cross gleamed, which the untrue
Yet innocent fair legends say,
Memorialises Christ our Lord
When Him with palms the throngs adored
Upon the foal. Many a year
The wanderer's heart had longed to view
Green banks of Jordan dipped in dew ;
Oft had he watched with starting tear
Pack-mule and camel, horse and spear,
Monks, soldiers, pilgrims, helm and hood,
The variegated annual train
In vernal Easter caravan,
Bound unto Gilgal's neighbourhood.
Nor less belief his heart confessed
Not die he should till knees had pressed
The Palmers' Beach. Which trust proved true,
'Twas charity gave faith her due :
Without publicity or din
It was the student moved herein.

He, Clarel, with the earnest face
Which fitful took a hectic dye,
Kept near the saint. With equal pace
Came Rolfe in saddle pommelled high,
Yet e'en behind that peaked redoubt
Sat Indian-like, in pliant way,
As if he were an Osage scout,
Or Gaucho of the Paraguay.

Lagging in rear of all the train
As hardly he pertained thereto
Or his right place therein scarce knew,
Rode one who frequent turned again
To pore behind. He seemed to be
In reminiscence folded ever,
Or some deep moral fantasy ;
At whiles in face a dusk and shiver,
As if in heart he heard amazed
The sighing of Ravenna's wood
Of pines, and saw the phantom knight
(Boccaccio's) with the dagger raised
Still hunt the lady in her flight
From solitude to solitude.
'Twas Vine. Nor less for day-dream, still
The rein he held with lurking will.

So filed the muster whose array
Threaded the Dolorosa's way.

II

THE SKULL-CAP

'SEE him in his uncheerful head-piece !
Libertad's on the Mexic coin
Would better suit me for a shade-piece :
Ah, had I known he was to join ! '—
    So chid the Greek, the banker one,
Perceiving Mortmain there at hand,
And in allusion to a dun
Skull-cap he wore. Derwent light reined
The steed ; and thus : ' Beg pardon, now,
It looks a little queer, concede ;
Nor less the cap fits well-shaped brow ;
It yet may prove the wishing-cap
Of Fortunatus.'
              ' No, indeed,
No, no, for *that* had velvet nap
Of violet with silver tassel—
Much like my smoking-cap, you see,'
Light laughed the Smyrniote, that vassal
Of health and young vivacity.
    ' Glaucon, be still,' the senior said
(And yet he liked to hear him too) ;
' I say it doth but ill bestead
To have a black cap in our crew.'
    ' Pink, pink,' cried Glaucon, ' pink 's the
        hue :—

      ' Pink cap and ribbons of the pearl,
        A Paradise of bodice,
      The Queen of Sheba's laundry girl—

'Hallo, what now ?   They come to halt
Down here in glen !   Well, well, we 'll vault.'
His song arrested, so he spake
And light dismounted, wide awake.—

'A sprightly comrade have you here,
Said Derwent in the senior's ear.
The banker turned him : ' Folly, folly—
But good against the melancholy.'

III

SHEEP-TRACKS they 'd look, at distance seen,
Did any herbage border them,
Those slender footpaths slanting lean
Down or along waste slopes which hem
The high-lodged, walled Jerusalem.
　　Slipped from Bethesda's Pool leads one
Which by an arch across is thrown
Kedron the brook.　The Virgin's Tomb
(Whence the near gate the Latins name—
St. Stephen's, as the Lutherans claim—
Hard by the place of martyrdom),
Time-worn in sculpture dim, is set
Humbly inearthed by Olivet.
　　'Tis hereabout now halt the band,
And by Gethsemane at hand,
For few omitted trifles wait
And guardsman whom adieus belate.
Some light dismount.
　　　　　　　　　　But hardly here,
Where on the verge they might foretaste
Or guess the flavour of the waste,
Greek sire and son took festive cheer.
　　Glaucon not less a topic found
At venture.　One old tree becharmed
Leaned its decrepit trunk deformed
Over the garden's wayside bound :
' See now : this yellow olive wood
They carve in trinkets—rosary—rood :

181

Of these we must provide some few
For travel-gifts, ere we for good
Set out for home.   And why not too
Some of those gems the nuns revere—
In hands of veteran venders here,
Wrought from the Kedron's saffron block
In the Monk's Glen, Mar Saba's rock ;
And cameos of the Dead Sea stone ? '
   ' Buy what ye will, be it Esau's flock,'
The other said : ' but for that stone—
Avoid, nor name ! '
                ' *That* stone ? what one ? '
And cast a look of grieved surprise
Marking the senior's ruffled guise ;
' Those cameos of Death's Sea——'
                    ' Have done,
I beg !   Unless all joy you 'd cripple,
Both noun omit and participle.'
   ' Dear sir, what noun ? strange grammar 's this.'
' Have I expressed myself amiss ?
Oh, don't you think it is but spleen :
A well-bred man counts it unclean
This name of—boy, and can't you guess ?
Last bankruptcy without redress ! '
   ' For heaven's sake ! '
                  ' With that ill word
Whose first is D and last is Ľ,
No matter what be in regard,
Let none of mine ere crape his speech,
But shun it, ay, and shun the knell
Of each derivative.'
             ' Oh, well—
I see, I see ; with all my heart !
Each conjugation will I curb,
All moods and tenses of the verb ;

And, for the noun, to save from errors
I 'll use instead—the " *King of Terrors.*" '
      ' Sir, change the topic.—Would 'twere done,
This scheme of ours, and we clean gone
From out this same dull land so holy
Which breeds but blues and melancholy.
To while our waiting I thought good
To join these travellers on their road ;
But there 's a bird in saucy glee
Trills—*Fool, retreat ; 'tis not for thee.*
Had I fair pretext now, I 'd turn.
But yonder—*he* don't show concern,'
Glancing toward Derwent, lounging there
Holding his horse with easy air
Slack by the rein.
                              With morning zest,
In sound digestion unoppressed,
The clergyman's good spirits made
A Tivoli of that grim glade.
And turning now his cheery eyes
Toward Salem's towers in solemn guise
Stretched dumb along the Mount of God,
He cried to Clarel waiting near
In saddle-seat and gazing drear :
' A canter, lad, on steed clean-shod
Didst ever take on English sod ?
The downs, the downs !   Yet even here
For a fair matin ride withal
I like the run round yonder wall.
Height have you, outlook ; and the view
Varies as you the turn pursue.'—
So he, thro' inobservance, blind
To that preoccupied young mind,
In frame how different, in sooth—
Pained and reverting still to Ruth

Immured and parted from him there
Behind those ramparts of despair.
　　Mortmain, whose wannish eyes declared
How ill thro' night hours he had fared,
By chance overheard, and muttered—' Brass,
A sounding brass and tinkling cymbal !
Who he that with a tongue so nimble
Affects light heart in such a pass ? '
And full his cloud on Derwent bent :
' Yea, and but thou seem'st well content.
But turn, another thing 's to see :
Thy back 's upon Gethsemane.'
　　The priest wheeled short :　What kind of man
Was this ?　The other re-began :
' 'Tis *Terra Santa*—Holy Land :
Terra Damnata though 's at hand
Within.'—' You mean where Judas stood ?
Yes, monks locate and name that ground ;
They 've railed it off.　Good, very good :
It minds one of a vacant pound.—
We tarry long :　why lags our man ? '
And rose ;　anew glanced toward the height.
　　Here Mortmain from the words and plight
Conjecture drew ;　and thus he ran :
' Be some who with the god will sup,
Happy to share his paschal wine.
'Tis well.　But the ensuing cup,
The bitter cup ? '
　　　　　　　　' Art a divine ? '
Asked Derwent, turning that aside ;
' Methinks, good friend, too much you chide.
I know these precincts.　Still, believe—
And let 's discard each idle trope—
Rightly considered, they can give
A hope to man, a cheerful hope.'

'Not for this world. The Christian plea—
What basis has it, but that here
Man is not happy, nor can be ?
There it confirms philosophy :
The compensation of its cheer
Is reason why the grass survives
Of verdurous Christianity,
Ay, trampled, lives, tho' hardly thrives
In these mad days.'—
     Surprised at it,
Derwent intently viewed the man,
Marked the unsolaced aspect wan ;
And fidgeted ; yet matter fit
Had offered ; but the other changed
In quick caprice, and wilful ranged
In wild invective : ' O abyss !
Here, upon what was erst the sod,
A man betrayed the yearning god ;
A man, yet with a woman's kiss.
'Twas *human*, that unanimous cry,
" We 're fixed to hate Him—Crucify ! "
The which they did. And hands, nailed down,
Might not avail to screen the face
From each head-wagging, mocking one.
This day, with some of earthly race,
May passion similar go on ? '—
  Inferring, rightly or amiss,
Some personal peculiar cause
For such a poignant strain as this,
The priest disturbed not here the pause
Which sudden fell. The other turned,
And, with a strange transition, burned
Invokingly : ' Ye trunks of moan—
Gethsemane olives, do ye hear
The trump of that vainglorious land

Where human nature they enthrone,
Displacing the divine ? '   His hand
He raised there—let it fall, and fell
Himself, with the last syllable,
To moody hush.   Then, fierce : ' Hired band
Of laureates of man's fallen tribe—
Slaves are ye, slaves beyond the scribe
Of Nero ; he, if flatterer blind,
Toadied not total human kind,
Which ye kerns do.   But Bel shall bow
And Nebo stoop.'
       ' Ah, come, friend, come,'
Pleaded the charitable priest,
Still bearing with him, anyhow,
By fate unbidden to joy's feast :
' Thou 'rt strong ; yield then the weak some room.
Too earnest art thou ' ; and with eye
Of one who fain would mollify
All frowardness, he looked a smile.
  But not that heart might he beguile :
' Man 's vicious : snaffle him with kings ;
Or, if kings cease to curb, devise
Severer bit.   This garden brings
Such lesson.   Heed it, and be wise
In thoughts not new.'
       ' Thou 'rt ill to-day,'
Here peering, but in cautious way,
' Nor solace find in valley wild.'
  The other wheeled, nor more would say ;
And soon the cavalcade defiled.

IV

OF MORTMAIN

'OUR friend there—he's a little queer,'
To Rolfe said Derwent, riding on ;
'Beshrew me, there is in his tone
Naught of your new world's chanticleer.
Who's the eccentric ? can you say ? '
    'Partly ; but 'tis at second-hand.
At the Black Jew's I met with one
Who, in response to my demand,
Did in a strange disclosure run
Respecting him.'—'Repeat it, pray.'—
And Rolfe complied.   But here receive
Less the details of narrative
Than what the drift and import may convey.

    A Swede he was—illicit son
Of noble lady, after-wed,
Who, for a cause over which be thrown
Charity of oblivion dead,—
Bore little love, but rather hate,
Even practised to ensnare his state.
His father, while not owning, yet
In part discharged the natural debt
Of duty ; gave him liberal lore
And timely income ; but no more.
    Thus isolated, what to bind
But the vague bond of human kind ?

The north he left, to Paris came—
Paris, the nurse of many a flame
Evil and good.   This son of earth,
This Psalmanazer, made a hearth
In warm desires and schemes for man :
Even *he* was an Arcadian.
Peace and good will was his acclaim—
If not in words, yet in the aim :
Peace, peace on earth : that note he thrilled,
But scarce in way the cherubs trilled
To Bethlehem and the shepherd band.
Yet much his theory could tell ;
And he expounded it so well,
Disciples came.   He took his stand.
     Europe was in a decade dim :
Upon the future's trembling rim
The comet hovered.   His a league
Of frank debate and close intrigue :
Plot, proselyte, appeal, denounce—
Conspirator, pamphleteer, at once,
And prophet.   Wear and tear and jar
He met with coffee and cigar :
These kept awake the man and mood
And dream.   That uncreated Good
He sought, whose absence is the cause
Of creeds and Atheists, mobs and laws.
Precocities of heart outran
The immaturities of brain.
     Along with each superior mind,
The vain, foolhardy, worthless, blind,
With Judases, are nothing loath
To clasp pledged hands and take the oath
Of aim, the which, if just, demands
Strong hearts, brows deep, and priestly hands.
Experience with her sharper touch

Stung Mortmain :   Why, if men prove such,
Dote I ? love theory overmuch ?
Yea, also, whither will advance
This Revolution sprung in France
So many years ago ? where end ?
That current takes me.   Whither tend ?
Come, thou who makest such hot haste
To forge the future—weigh the past.
      Such frame he knew.   And timed event
Cogent a further question lent :
Wouldst meddle with the state ?   Well, mount
Thy guns ; how many men dost count ?
Besides, there 's more that here belongs :
Be many questionable wrongs :
By yet more questionable war,
Prophet of peace, these wouldst thou bar ?
The world 's not new, nor new thy plea.
Tho' even shouldst thou triumph, see,
Prose overtakes the victor's songs :
Victorious right may need redress :
No failure like a harsh success.
Yea, ponder well the historic page :
Of all who, fired with noble rage,
Have warred for right without reprieve,
How many spanned the wings immense
Of Satan's muster, or could cheat
His cunning tactics of retreat
And ambuscade ?   Oh, now dispense !
The world is portioned out, believe :
The good have but a patch at best,
The wise their corner ; for the rest—
Malice divides with ignorance.
And what is stable ? find one boon
That is not lackey to the moon
Of fate.   The flood ebbs out—the ebb

Floods back ; the incessant shuttle shifts
And flies, and wears and tears the web.
Turn, turn thee to the proof that sifts :
What if the kings in Forty-eight
Fled like the gods ? even as the gods
Shall do, return they made ; and sate
And fortified their strong abodes ;
And, to confirm them there in state,
Contrived new slogans, apt to please—
Pan and the tribal unities.
Behind all this still works some power
Unknowable, thou 'lt yet adore.
That steers the world, not man. States drive ;
The crazy rafts with billows strive.—
Go, go—absolve thee. Join that band
That wash them with the desert sand
For lack of water. In the dust
Of wisdom sit thee down, and rust.

So mused he—solitary pined.
Tho' his apostolate had thrown
New prospects ope to Adam's kind,
And fame had trumped him far and free—
Now drop he did—a clod unknown ;
Nay, rather, he would not disown
Oblivion's volunteer to be ;
Like those new world discoverers bold
Ending in stony convent cold,
Or dying hermits ; as if they,
Chastised to Micah's mind austere,
Remorseful felt that ampler sway
Their lead had given for old career
Of human nature.
          But this man
No cloister sought. He, under ban

Of strange repentance and last dearth,
Roved the gray places of the earth.
And what seemed most his heart to wring
Was some unrenderable thing :
'Twas not his bastardy, nor bale
Medean in his mother pale,
Nor thwarted aims of high design ;
But deeper—deep as nature's mine.
    Tho' frequent among kind he sate
Tranquil enough to hold debate,
His moods he had, mad fitful ones,
Prolonged or brief, outbursts or moans ;
And at such times would hiss or cry :
' Fair Circe—goddess of the sty ! '
More frequent this : ' Mock worse than wrong :
The Syren's kiss—the Fury's thong ! '

    Such he. Tho' scarce as such portrayed
In full by Rolfe, yet Derwent said
At close : ' There 's none so far astray,
Detached, abandoned, as might seem,
As to exclude the hope, the dream
Of fair redemption. One fine day
I saw at sea, by bit of deck—
Weedy—adrift from far away—
The dolphin in his gambol light,
Through showery spray, arch into sight :
He flung a rainbow o'er that wreck.'

V

CLAREL AND GLAUCON

Now slanting toward the mountain's head
They round its southern shoulder so ;
That immemorial path they tread
Whereby to Bethany you go
From Salem over Kedron's bed
And Olivet.   Free change was made
Among the riders.   Lightly strayed,
With overtures of friendly note,
To Clarel's side the Smyrniote.
    Wishful from every one to learn,
As well his giddy talk to turn,
Clarel—in simpleness that comes
To students versed more in their tomes
Than life—of Homer spake, a man
With Smyrna linked, born there, 'twas said.
But no, the light Ionian
Scarce knew that singing beggar dead,
Though wight he 'd heard of with the name ;
' Homer ? yes, I remember me ;
Saw note-of-hand once with his name :
A fig for him, fig-dealer he,
The veriest old nobody ' :
Then lightly skimming on : ' Did you
By Joppa come ?   I did, and rue
Three dumpish days, like Sundays dull
Such as in London late I knew ;
The gardens tho' are bountiful.

But Bethlehem—beyond compare !
Such roguish ladies !   Tarried there ?
You know it is a Christian town,
Decreed so under Ibrahim's rule,
The Turk.'   E'en thus he rippled on,
Way giving to his spirits free,
Relieved from that disparity
Of years he with the banker felt ;
Nor noted Clarel's puzzled look,
Who, novice-like, at first mistook,
Doubting lest satire might be dealt.
    Adjusting now the sporting gun
Slung to his back with pouch and all :
' Oh, but to sight a bird, just one,
An eagle say, and see him fall.'
And, chatting still, with giddy breath,
Of hunting feats over hill and dale :
' Fine shot was mine by Nazareth ;
But birding 's best in Tempe's Vale :
From Thessalonica, you know
'Tis thither that we fowlers stray.
But you don't talk, my friend.—Heigh-ho,
Next month I wed ; yes, so they say.
Meantime do sing a song or so
To cheer one.   Won't ?   Must I ?—Let 's see :
Song of poor-devil dandy : he :—

    ' She 's handsome as a jewelled priest
      In ephod on the festa,
  And each poor blade like me must needs
      Idolise and detest her.

    ' With rain-beads on her odorous hair
      From gardens after showers,
  All bloom and dew she trips along,
      Intent on selling flowers.

' She beams—the rainbow of the bridge ;
  But ah, my blank abhorrence,
She buttonholes me with a rose,
  This flower-girl of Florence.

' My friends stand by ; and, "There!" she says—
  An angel arch, a sinner :
I grudge to pay, but pay I must,
  Then—dine on half a dinner !—

  ' Heigh-ho, next month I marry : well ! '
With that he turned aside, and went
Humming another air content.
And Derwent heard him as befell.
' This lad is like a land of springs,'
He said, ' he gushes so with song.'—
' Nor heeds if Olivet it wrong,'
Said Rolfe ; ' but no—he sings—he rings ;
His is the guinea, fiddle-strings
Of youth too—which may heaven make strong ! '
    Meanwhile, in tetchy tone austere
That reprobated song and all,
Lowering rode the presbyter,
A cloud whose rain ere long must fall.

VI

THE HAMLET

In silence now they pensive win
A slope of upland over hill
Eastward, where heaven and earth be twin
In quiet, and earth seems heaven's sill.
About a hamlet there full low,
Nor cedar, palm, nor olive show—
Three trees by ancient legend claimed
As those whereof the cross was framed.
Nor dairy white, nor well-curb green,
Nor cheerful husbandry was seen,
Though flinty tillage might be named :
Nor less if all showed strange and lone
The peace of God seemed settled down :
Mary and Martha's mountain-town.

To Rolfe the priest said, breathing low :
' How placid !   Carmel's beauty here,
If added, could not more endear.'—
Rolfe spake not, but he bent his brow.

Aside glanced Clarel on the face
Of meekness ; and he mused : In thee
Methinks similitude I trace
To Nature's look in Bethany.
But, ah, and can one dream the dream
That hither thro' the shepherds' gate,
Even by the road we travelled late,
Came Jesus from Jerusalem,

Who pleased Him so in fields and bowers,
Yes, crowned with thorns, still loved the flowers ?
Poor gardeners here that turned the sod
Friends were they to the Son of God ?
And shared He e'en their humble lot ?
The sisters here in pastoral plot
Green to the door—did they yield rest,
And bathe the feet, and spread the board
For Him, their own and brother's guest,
The kindly Christ, even man's fraternal Lord ?
But see : how with a wandering hand,
In absent-mindedness afloat,
And dreaming of his fairyland,
Nehemiah smooths the ass's coat.

VII

DESCENDING by the mountain-side
When crags give way to pastures wide,
And lower opening, ever new,
Glades, meadows, hamlets meet the view,
Which from above did coyly hide—
And with rekindled breasts of spring
The robins thro' the orchard wing ;
Excellent then—as *there* bestowed—
And true in charm the downward road.
Quite other spells an influence throw
Down going, down, to Jericho.
    Here first on path so evil-starred
Their guide they scan, and prize the guard.

    The guide, a Druze of Lebanon,
Was rumoured for an Emir's son,
Or offspring of a lord undone
In Ibrahim's time. Abrupt reverse
The princes in the East may know :
Lawgivers are outlaws at a blow,
And Crœsus dwindles in the purse.
Exiled, cut off, in friendless state,
The Druze maintained an air sedate ;
Without the sacrifice of pride,
Sagacious still he earned his bread,
E'en managed to maintain the head,
Yes, lead men still, if but as guide
To pilgrims.

Here his dress to mark :
A simple woollen cloak, with dark
Vertical stripes ; a vest to suit ;
White turban like snow-wreath ; a boot
Exempt from spur ; a sash of fair
White linen, long-fringed at the ends :
The garb of Lebanon.   His mare
In keeping showed : the saddle plain :
Headstall untasseled, slender rein.
But nature made her rich amends
For art's default : full eye of flame
Tempered in softness, which became
Womanly sometimes, in desire
To be caressed ; ears fine to know
Least intimation, catch a hint
As tinder takes the spark from flint
And steel.   Veil-like her clear attire
Of silvery hair, with speckled show
Of grayish spots, and ample flow
Of milky mane.   Much like a child
The Druze she 'd follow, more than mild.
Not less, at need, what power she 'd don,
Clothed with the thunderbolt would run
As conscious of the Emir's son
She bore ; nor knew the hireling's lash,
Red rowel, or rebuke as rash.
Courteous her treatment.   But deem not
This tokened a luxurious lot :
Her diet spare ; sole stable, earth ;
Beneath the burning sun she 'd lie
With mane dishevelled, whence her eye
Would flash across the fiery dearth,
As watching for that other queen,
Her mate, a beauteous Palmyrene,
The pride of Tadmore's tented scene.

Athwart the pommel-cloth coarse-spun
A long pipe lay, and longer gun,
With serviceable yataghan.
But prized above these arms of yore,
A new revolver bright he bore
Tucked in the belt, and oft would scan.
Accoutred thus, thro' desert-blight
Whose lord is the Amalekite,
And proffering or peace or war,
The swart Druze rode his silvery Zar.

Behind him, jogging two and two,
Came troopers six of tawny hue,
Bewrinkled veterans, and grave
As Carmel's prophets of the cave :
Old Arab Bethlehemites, with guns
And spears of grandsires old. Weird ones,
Their robes like palls funereal hung
Down from the shoulder, one fold flung
In mufflement about the head,
And kept there by a fillet's braid.

Over this venerable troop
Went Belex doughty in command,
Erst of the Sultan's saucy troop
Which into death he did disband—
Politic Mahmoud—when that clan
By fair pretence, in festive way,
He trapped within the Artmedan—
Of old, Byzantium's circus gay.
But Belex a sultana saved—
His senior, though by love enslaved,
Who fed upon the stripling's May—
Long since, for now his beard was gray ;
Tho' goodly yet the features fine,

Firm chin, true lip, nose aquiline—
Type of the pure Osmanli breed.
But ah, equipments gone to seed—
Ah, shabby fate ! his vesture's cloth
Hinted the Jew bazaar and moth :
The saddle, too, a cast-off one,
An Aga's erst, and late was sown
With seed-pearl in the seat ; but now
All that, with tag-work, all was gone—
The tag-work of wee bells in row
That made a small, snug, dulcet din
About the housings Damascene.
But mark the bay : his twenty years
Still showed him pawing with his peers.
Pure desert air, doled diet pure,
Sleek tendance, brave result insure.
Ample his chest ; small head, large eye—
How interrogative with soul—
Responsive too, his master by :
Trim hoof, and pace in strong control.

    Thy birthday well they keep, thou Don,
And well thy birthday ode they sing ;
Nor ill they named thee Solomon,
Prolific sire.   Long live the king.

VIII

THEY journey. And, as heretofore,
Derwent invoked his spirits bright
Against the wilds expanding more :
   ' Do but regard yon Islamite
And horse : equipments be but lean,
Nor less the nature still is rife—
Mettle, you see, mettle and mien.
Methinks fair lesson here we glean :
The inherent vigour of man's life
Transmitted from strong Adam down,
Takes no infirmity that 's won
By institutions—which, indeed,
Be as equipments of the breed.
God bless the marrow in the bone !
What 's Islam now ? does Turkey thrive ?
Yet Islamite and Turk they wive
And flourish, and the world goes on.'
   ' Ay. But all qualities of race
Which make renown—these yet may die,
While leaving unimpaired in grace
The virile power,' was Rolfe's reply ;
' For witness here I cite a Greek—
God bless him ! who tricked me of late
In Argos. What a perfect beak
In contour—oh, 'twas delicate ;
And hero-symmetry of limb :
Clownish I looked by side of him.

201

Oh, but it does one's ardour damp—
That splendid instrument, a scamp !
These Greeks indeed they wear the kilt
Bravely ; they skim their lucid seas ;
But, prithee, where is Pericles ?
Plato is where ?   Simonides ?
No, friend : much good wine has been spilt :
The rank world prospers ; but, alack !
Eden nor Athens shall come back :—
And what 's become of Arcady ? '
    He paused ; then in another key :
' Prone, prone are era, man and nation
To slide into a degradation !
With some, to age is that—but that.'

    ' Pathetic grow'st thou,' Derwent said :
And lightly, as in leafy glade,
Lightly he in the saddle sat.

IX

In order meet they take their way
Through Bahurim where David fled ;
And Shimei like a beast of prey
Prowled on the side-cliff overhead,
And flung the stone, the stone and curse,
And called it just, the king's reverse :
Still grieving grief, as demons may.

In flanking parched ravine they won,
The student wondered at the bale
So arid, as of Acheron
Run dry.   Alert showed Belex hale,
Uprising in the stirrup, clear
Of saddle, outlook so to gain.
Rattling his piece and scimetar.
    ' Dear me, I say,' appealing ran
From the sleek Thessalonian.
    ' Say on ! ' the Turk, with bearded grin ;
' This is the glen named Adommin ! '
    Uneasy glance the banker threw,
Tho' first now of such name he knew
Or place.   Nor was his flutter stayed
When Belex, heading his brigade,
Drew sword, and with a summons cried :
' Ho, rout them ! ' and his cohort veered,
Scouring the dens on either side,
Then all together disappeared

203

Amid wild turns of ugly ground
Which well the sleuth-dog might confound.
　　The Druze, as if 'twere nothing new—
The Turk doing but as bid to do—
A higher standpoint would command ;
　　But here across his shortened rein
And loosened, shrewd, keen yataghan,
Good Nehemiah laid a hand :
' Djalea, stay—not long I 'll be ;
A word, one Christian word with ye.
I 've just been reading in the place
How, on a time, carles far from grace
Left here half-dead the faring man :
Those wicked thieves.　But Heaven befriends,
Still Heaven at need a rescue lends :
Mind ye the Good Samaritan ? '—
　　In patient self-control high-bred,
Half of one sense, an ear, the Druze
Inclined ;　the while his grave eye fed
Afar ;　his arms at hand for use.
　　' He,' said the meek one, going on,
Naught heeding but the tale he spun,
' He, when he saw him in the snare,
He had compassion ;　and with care
Him gently wakened from the swound
And oil and wine poured in the wound ;
Then set him on his own good beast,
And bare him to the nighest inn—
A man not of his town or kin—
And tended whom he thus released ;
Up with him sat he all that night,
Put off he did his journey quite ;
And on the morrow, ere he went,
For the mistrustful host he sent,
And taking out his careful purse,

He gave him pence ; and thus did sue :
" Beseech ye now that well ye nurse
This poor man whom I leave with you ;
And whatsoe'er thou spendest more,
When I again come, I 'll restore."—
Ye mind the chapter ?   Well, this day
Were some forlorn one here to bleed,
Aid would be meted to his need
In good soul travelling this way.
Speak I amiss ? an answer, pray ? '—
 In deference the armed man,
O'er pistols, gun, and yataghan,
The turban bowed, but nothing said ;
Then turned—resumed his purpose.   Led
By old traditionary sense,
A liberal, fair reverence,
The Orientals homage pay,
And licence yield in tacit way
To men demented, or so deemed.

 Derwent meanwhile in saddle there
Heard all, but scarce at ease he seemed,
So ill the tale and time did pair.

 Vine whispered to the saint aside :
' There was a Levite and a priest.'
 ' Whom God forgive,' he mild replied,
' As I forget ' ; and there he ceased.

 Touching that trouble in advance,
Some here, much like to landsmen wise
At sea in hour which tackle tries,
The adventure's issue left to chance.
 In spent return the escort wind
Reporting they had put to flight

Some prowlers.—' Look ! ' one cried.   Behind
A lesser ridge just glide from sight—
Though neither man nor horse appears—
Steel points and hair-tufts of five spears.
Like dorsal fins of sharks they show
When upright these divide the wave
And peer above, while down in grave
Of waters, slide the body lean
And charnel mouth.

       With thoughtful mien
The student fared, nor might withstand
The something dubious in the Holy Land.

X

In divers ways which vary it,
Stones mention find in hallowed Writ :
Stones rolled from well-mouths, altar stones,
Idols of stone, memorial ones,
Sling-stones, stone tables ; Bethel high
Saw Jacob, under starry sky,
On stones his head lay—desert bones ;
Stones sealed the sepulchres—huge cones
Heaved there in bulk ; death too by stones
The law decreed for crime ; in spite
As well, for taunt, or type of ban,
The same at place were cast, or man ;
Or piled upon the pits of fight
Reproached or even denounced the slain :
So in the wood of Ephraim, some
Laid the great heap over Absalom.

    Convenient too at wilful need,
Stones prompted many a ruffian deed
And ending oft in parting groans :
By stones died Naboth ; stoned to death
Was Stephen meek : and Scripture saith,
Against even Christ they took up stones.

    Moreover, as a thing profuse,
Suggestive still in every use,
On stones, still stones, the Gospels dwell
In lesson meet or happier parable.

207

Attesting here the Holy Writ—
In brook, in glen, by tomb and town
In natural way avouching it—
Behold the stones ! And never one
A lichen greens ; and, turn them o'er—
No worm—no life : but, all the more,
Good witnesses.

            The way now led
Where shoals of flints and stones lay dead.
The obstructed horses tripped and stumbled,
The Thessalonian groaned and grumbled.

    But Glaucon cried : ' Alack the stones !
Or be they pilgrims' broken bones
Wherewith they pave the turnpikes here ?
Is this your sort of world, Mynheer ?

    ' Not on your knee—no no, no no ;
      But sit you so : verily and verily,
    Paris, are you true or no ?
      I 'll look down your eyes and see.

    ' Helen, look—and look and look ;
      Look me, Helen, through and through ;
    Make me out the only rake :
      Set down one and carry two.'—

    ' Have done, sir,' roared the Elder out ;
' Have done with this lewd balladry.'—
    Amazed the singer turned about ;
But when he saw that, past all doubt,
The Scot was in dead earnest, he,
' Oh now, monsieur—monsieur, monsieur ! '
Appealing there so winningly—
Conceding, as it were, his age,
Station, and moral gravity,

And right to be morose indeed,
Nor less endeavouring to assuage
At least.   But scarce did he succeed.

Rolfe likewise, if in other style,
Here sought that hard road to beguile :
' The stone was man's first missile ; yes,
Cain hurled it, or his sullen hand
Therewith made heavy.   Cain, confess,
A savage was, although he planned
His altar.   Altars such as Cain's
Still find we on far island-chains
Deep mid the woods and hollows dark,
And set off like the shittim Ark.
Refrain from trespass ; with black frown
Each votary straight takes up his stone—
As once against even me indeed :
I see them now start from their rocks
In malediction.'
                          ' Yet concede,
They were but touchy in their creed,'
Said Derwent ; ' but did you succumb ?
These irritable orthodox ! '—
         Thereat the Elder waxed more glum.

A halt being called now with design
Biscuit to bite and sip the wine,
The student saw the turbaned Druze
A courtesy peculiar use
In act of his accosting Vine,
Tho' but in trifle—as to how
The saddle suited.   And before,
In little things, he 'd marked the show
Of like observance.   How explore
The cause of this, and understand ?

The pilgrims were an equal band :
Why this preferring way toward one ?
    But Rolfe explained in undertone :
' But few, believe, have nicer eye
For the cast of aristocracy
Than Orientals. Well now, own,
Despite at times a manner shy,
Shows not our countryman in mould
Of a romanced nobility ?
His chary speech, his rich still air
Confirm them in conjecture there.
I make slim doubt these people hold
Vine for some lord who fain would go,
For delicate cause, incognito.—
What means Sir Crab ? '—
                            In smouldering ire
The Elder, not dismounting, views
The nearer prospect ; ill content,
The distance next his glance pursues,
A land of Eblis burned with fire ;
Recoils ; then, with big eyebrows bent,
Lowers on the comrades—Derwent most,
With luncheon now and flask engrossed ;
His bridle turns, adjusts his seat
And holsters where the pistols be,
Nor taking leave like Christian sweet
(Quite mindless of Paul's courtesy),
With dumb indomitable chin
Straight back he aims thro' Adommin,
Alone, nor blandly self-sustained—
Robber and robber-glen disdained.

    As stiff he went, his humour dark
From Vine provoked a vivid spark—
Derisive comment, part restrained.
    He passes. Well, peace with him go.

If truth have painted heart but grim,
None here hard measure meant for him ;
Nay, Haytian airs around him blow,
And woo and win to cast behind
The harsher and inclement mind.
But needs narrate what followed now.
    ' Part from us,' Derwent cried, ' that way ?
I fear we have offended. Nay,
What other cause ? '—
                    ' The desert, see :
He and the desert don't agree,'
Said Rolfe ; ' or rather, let me say
He can't provoke a quarrel here
With blank indifference so drear :
Ever the desert waives dispute,
Cares not to argue, bides but mute.
Besides, no topographic cheer :
Surveyor's tape don't come in play ;
The same with which upon a day
He upon all fours soused did roam
Measuring the sub-ducts of Siloam.
Late asking him in casual way
Something about the Tomb's old fane,
These words I got : " Sir, I don't know ;
But once I dropped in—not again ;
'Tis monkish, 'tis a raree-show—
A raree-show. Saints, sites, and stuff.
Had I my will I 'd strip it, strip ! "
I knew 'twere vain to try rebuff ;
But asked, " Did Paul, embarked in ship
With Castor and Pollux for a sign,
Deem it incumbent there to rip
From stern and prow the name and shrine ? "
" Saint Paul, sir, had not zeal enough ;
I always thought so " ; and went on :

" Where stands this fane, this Calvary one
Alleged ? why, sir, *within* the site
Of Herod's wall ? Can *that* be right ? "
But why detail. Suffice, in few,
Even Zion's hill, he doubts that too ;
Nay, Sinai in his dry purview
He 's dubious if, as placed, it meet
Requirements.'

           ' Why then do his feet
Tread Judah ? no good end is won,'
Said Derwent.

           ' Curs need have a bone
To mumble, though but dry nor sweet.
Nay, that 's too harsh and overdone.
'Tis still a vice these carpers brew—
They try us—us set carping too.'

     ' Ah well, quick then in thought we 'll shun
         him,
And so foreclose all strictures on him.
Howbeit, this confess off-hand :
Amiss is robed in gown and band
A disenchanter.—Friend, the wine ! '

     The banker passed it without word.
Sad looked he : Why, these fools are stirred
About a nothing !—Plain to see
Such comradeship did ill agree :
Pedants, and poor ! nor used to dine
In ease of table-talk benign—
Steeds, pictures, ladies, gold, Tokay,
Gardens and baths, the English news,
Stamboul, the market—gain or lose ?

     He turned to where young Glaucon lay,
Who now to startled speech was won :
' Look, is he crazy ? see him there ! '
The saint it was with busy care

Flinging aside stone after stone,
Yet feebly, nathless, as he wrought
In charge imposed though not unloved ;
While every stone that he removed
Laid bare but more.   The student sighed,
So well he kenned his ways distraught
At influx of his eldritch tide.

  But Derwent, hastening to the spot,
Exclaimed, ' How now ? surely 'tis not
To mend the way ? '

       With patient look,
Poising a stone as 'twere a clod :
' All things are possible with God ;
The humblest helper will He brook.'

  Derwent stood dumb ; but quick in heart
Conjecturing how it was, addressed
Some friendly words, and slid apart ;
And, yet while by that scene impressed,
Came, as it chanced, where unbecalmed
Mortmain aloof sat all disarmed—
Legs lengthwise crossed, head hanging low,
The skull-cap pulled upon the brow,
Hands groping toward the knees : ' Then where ?
A Thug, the swordfish roams the sea—
The falcon 's pirate in the air ;
Betwixt the twain, where shalt thou flee,
Poor flying-fish ? whither repair ?
What other element for thee ?
Whales, mighty whales have felt the wound—
Plunged bleeding thro' the blue profound ;
But where their fangs the sand-sharks keep
Be shallows worse than any deep.'—

  Hardly that chimed with Derwent's bell :
Him too he left.

    When it befell

That new they started on their way ;
To turn the current or allay,
He talked with Clarel, and first knew
Nehemiah's conceit about the Jew :
The ways prepared, the tilth restored
For the second coming of Our Lord.
    Rolfe overheard : ' And shall we say
That this is craze ? or but, in brief,
Simplicity of plain belief ?
The early Christians, how did they ?
For His return looked any day.'

    From dwelling on Rolfe's thought, ere long
On Rolfe himself the student broods :
Surely I would not think a wrong ;
Nor less I 've shrunk from him in moods.
A bluntness is about him set :
Truth's is it ? But he winneth yet
Through taking qualities which join.
Make these the character ? the rest
But rim ? On Syracusan coin
The barbarous letters shall invest
The relievo's infinite of charm.—
I know not. Does he help, or harm ?

XI

OF DESERTS

THO' frequent in the Arabian waste
The pilgrim, up ere dawn of day,
Inhale thy wafted musk, Cathay ;
And Adam's primal joy may taste,
Beholding all the pomp of night
Bee'd thick with stars in swarms how bright ;
And so, rides on alert and braced—
Tho' brisk at morn the pilgrim start,
Ere long he 'll know in weary hour
Small love of deserts, if their power
Make to retreat upon the heart
Their own forsakenness.
                          Darwin quotes
From Shelley, that forever floats
Over all desert places known,
Mysterious doubt—an awful one.
He quotes, adopts it. Is it true ?
Let instinct vouch ; let poetry,
Science and instinct here agree,
For truth requires strong retinue.

Waste places are where yet is given
A charm, a beauty from the heaven
Above them, and clear air divine—
Translucent ether opaline ;
And some in evening's early dew
Put on illusion of a guise
Which Tantalus might tantalise
Afresh ; ironical unrolled

Like Western counties all in grain
Ripe for the sickleman and wain ;
Or, tawnier than the Guinea gold,
More like a lion's skin unfold :
Attest the desert opening out
Direct from Cairo by the Gate
Of Victors, whence the annual rout
To Mecca bound, precipitate
Their turbaned frenzy.—
                Sands immense
Impart the oceanic sense :
The flying grit like scud is made :
Pillars of sand which whirl about
Or arc along in colonnade,
True kin be to the waterspout.
Yonder on the horizon, red
With storm, see there the caravan
Straggling long-drawn, dispirited ;
Mark how it labours like a fleet
Dismasted, which the cross-winds fan
In crippled disaster of retreat
From battle.—
                Sinai had renown
Ere thence was rolled the thundered Law ;
Ever a terror wrapped its crown ;
Never did shepherd dare to draw
Too nigh (Josephus saith) for awe
Of one, some ghost or god austere—
Hermit unknown, dread mountaineer.—

When comes the sun up over Nile
In cloudlessness, what cloud is cast
O'er Lybia ?   Thou shadow vast
Of Cheops' indissoluble pile,
Typ'st thou the imperishable Past

In empire posthumous and reaching sway
Projected far across to time's remotest day ?
    But curb.—Such deserts in air-zone
Or object lend suggestive tone,
Redeeming them.
                For Judah here—
Let Erebus her rival own :
'Tis horror absolute—severe,
Dead, livid, honeycombed, dumb, fell—
A caked depopulated hell ;
Yet so created, judged by sense,
And visaged in significance
Of settled anger terrible.
    Profoundly cloven through the scene
Winds Kedron—word (the scholar saith)
Importing anguish hard on death.
And aptly may such named ravine
Conduct unto Lot's mortal Sea
In cleavage from Gethsemane
Where it begins.
              But why does man
Regard religiously this tract
Cadaverous and under ban
Of blastment ? Nay, recall the fact
That in the pagan era old,
When bolts, deemed Jove's, tore up the mound,
Great stones the simple peasant rolled
And built a wall about the gap
Deemed hallowed by the thunder-clap.
So here : men here adore this ground
Which doom hath smitten. 'Tis a land
Direful yet holy—blest tho' banned.

    But to pure hearts it yields no fear ;
And John, he found wild honey here.

XII

THE BANKER

INFER the wilds which next pertain.
Though travel here be still a walk,
Small heart was theirs for easy talk.
Oblivious of the bridle-rein
Rolfe fell to Lethe altogether,
Bewitched by that uncanny weather
Of sultry cloud.   And home-sick grew
The banker.   In his revery blue
The cigarette, a summer friend,
Went out between his teeth—could lend
No solace, soothe him nor engage.
And now disrelished he each word
Of sprightly, harmless persiflage
Wherewith young Glaucon here would fain
Evince a jaunty disregard.
But hush betimes o'ertook the twain—
The more impressive, it may be,
For that the senior, somewhat spent,
Florid overmuch and corpulent,
Laboured in lungs, and audibly.

Rolfe, noting that the sufferer's steed
Was far less easy than his own,
Relieved him in his hour of need
By changing with him ; then in tone
Aside, half musing, as alone,
' Unwise he is to venture here,
Poor fellow ; 'tis but sorry cheer

For Mammon.   Ill would it accord
If nabob with asthmatic breath
Lighted on Holbein's Dance of Death
Sly slipped among his prints from Claude.
Cosmetic-users scarce are bold
To face a skull.   That sachem old
Whose wigwam is man's heart within—
How taciturn, and yet can speak,
Imparting more than volumes win ;
Not Pleasure's darling cares to seek
Such counsellor : the worse he fares ;
Since—heedless, taken unawares—
Arrest he finds.—Look : at yon ground
How starts he now !   So Abel's hound,
Snuffing his prostrate master wan,
Shrank back from earth's first murdered
        man.—
But friend, how thrivest ? ' turning there
To Derwent.   He, with altered air,
Made vague rejoinder, nor serene :
His soul, if not cast down, was vexed
By Nature in this dubious scene :
His theory she harsh perplexed—
The more so for wild Mortmain's mien :
And Nehemiah in eldritch cheer :
' Lord, now Thou goest forth from Seir ;
Lord, now from Edom marchest Thou ! '—

        Shunning the Swede—disturbed to know
The saint in strange clairvoyance so,
Clarel yet turned to meet the grace
Of one who not infected dwelt—
Yes, Vine, who shared his horse's pace
In level sameness, as both felt
At home in dearth.

But unconcern
That never knew Vine's thoughtful turn
The venerable escort showed :
True natives of the waste abode,
They moved like insects of the leaf—
Tint, tone adapted to the fief.

XIII

'KING, who betwixt the cross and sword
On ashes died in cowl and cord—
In desert died ; and, if thy heart
Betrayed thee not, from life didst part
A martyr for thy martyred Lord ;
Anointed one and undefiled—
O warrior manful, tho' a child
In simple faith—St. Louis ! rise,
And teach us out of holy eyes
Whence came thy trust.'

So Rolfe, and shrank,
Awed by that region dread and great ;
Thence led to take to heart the fate
Of one who tried in such a blank,
Believed—and died.
                    Lurching was seen
An Arab tall, on camel lean,
Up labouring from a glen's remove,
His long lance upright fixed above
The gun across the knee in guard.
So rocks in hollow trough of sea
A wreck with one gaunt mast, and yard
Displaced and slanting toward the lee.
Closer he drew ; with visage mute,
Austere in passing made salute.

221

Such courtesy may vikings lend
Who through the dreary Hela wend.
　　　Under gun, lance, and scabbard hacked
Pressed Nehemiah ; with ado
High he reached up an Arab tract
From the low ass—' Christ's gift to you ! '
With clatter of the steel he bore
The lofty nomad bent him o'er
In grave regard.　The camel too
Her crane-like neck swerved round to
　　　　view ;
Nor more to camel than to man
Inscrutable the ciphers ran.
But wonted unto arid cheer,
The beast, misjudging, snapped it up,
And would have munched, but let it drop ;
Her master, poling down his spear
Transfixed the page and brought it near,
Nor stayed his travel.
　　　　　　　　　On they went
Through solitudes, till made intent
By small sharp shots which stirred rebound
In echo.　Over upland drear
On tract of less obstructed ground
Came fairly into open sight
A mounted train in tulip plight :
Ten Turks, whereof advanced rode four,
With levelled pistols, left and right
Graceful diverging, as in plume
Feather from feather.　So brave room
They make for turning toward each shore
Ambiguous in nooks of blight,
Discharging shots ;　then reunite,
And, with obeisance bland, adore
Their prince, a fair youth, who, behind—

'Tween favourites of equal age,
Brilliant in paynim equipage—
With Eastern dignity how sweet,
Nods to their homage, pleased to mind
Their gallant curvets. Still they meet,
Salute and wheel, and him precede,
As in a pleasure-park or mead.

    The escorts join ; and some would
        take
To parley, as is wont. The Druze,
Howbeit, hardly seems to choose
The first advances here to make ;
Nor does he shun.   Alert is seen
One in voluminous turban green,
Beneath which in that barren place
Sheltered he looks as by the grace
Of shady palm-tuft. Vernal he
In sacerdotal chivalry :
That turban by its hue declares
That the great Prophet's blood he shares :
Kept as the desert stallions be,
'Tis an attested pedigree.
But ah, the bigot, he could lower
In mosque on the intrusive Giaour.
To make him truculent for creed
Family pride joined personal greed.
    Tho' foremost here his word he vents—
Officious in the conference,
In rank and sway he ranged, in sooth,
Behind that fine sultanic youth
Which held his place apart, and, cool,
In lapse or latency of rule
Seemed mindless of the halting train
And pilgrims there of Franquestan

Or land of Franks.   Remiss he wore
An indolent look superior.
His grade might justify the air :
The viceroy of Damascus' heir.
His father's jurisdiction sweeps
From Lebanon to Ammon's steeps.
Return he makes from mission far
To independent tribes of war
Beyond the Houran.   In advance
Of the main escort, gun and lance,
He aims for Salem back.

                   This learned,
In anxiousness the banker yearned
To join ; nor Glaucon seemed averse.
'Twas quick resolved, and soon arranged
Through fair diplomacy of purse
And Eastern compliments exchanged.
    Their wine, in pannier of the mule,
Upon the pilgrims they bestow :
' And pledge us, friends, in valley cool,
If such this doleful road may know :
Farewell ! '   And so the Moslem train
Received these Christians, happy twain.

    They fled.   And thou ?   The way is
        dun ;
Why further follow the Emir's son ?
Scarce yet the thought may well engage
To lure thee thro' these leafless bowers,
That little avails a pilgrimage
Whose road but winds among the flowers.
Part here, then, would ye win release
From ampler dearth ; part, and in peace.
Nay, part like Glaucon, part with song :
The note receding dies along :

'Tarry never there
Where the air
Lends a lone Hadean spell—
Where the ruin and the wreck
Vine and ivy never deck,
And wizard wan and sibyl dwell :
There, oh, beware !

'Rather seek the grove—
Thither rove,
Where the leaf that falls to ground
In a violet upsprings,
And the oracle that sings
Is the bird above the mound :
There, tarry there ! '

XIV

BY ACHOR

JERUSALEM, the mountain town,
Is based how far above the sea ;
But down, a lead-line's long reach down,
A deep-sea lead, beneath the zone
Of ocean's level, Heaven's decree
Has sunk the pool whose deeps submerged
The doomed Pentapolis fire-scourged.

    Long then the slope, though varied oft,
From Zion to the seats abject ;
For rods and roods ye wind aloft
By verges where the pulse is checked ;
And chief both height and steepness show
Ere Achor's gorge the barrier rends
And like a thunder-cloud impends
Ominous over Jericho.

    Hard by the brink the Druze leads on,
But halts at a projecting crown
Of cliff, and beckons them.   Nor goat
Nor fowler ranging far and high
Scales such a steep ; nor vulture's eye
Scans one more lone.   Deep down in throat
It shows a sooty black.
                ' A forge
Abandoned,' Rolfe said, ' thus may look.'
    ' Yea,' quoth the saint, ' and read the
        Book :
Flames, flames have forked in Achor's gorge.'
226

His wizard vehemence surprised ;
Some new illusion they surmised ;
Not less authentic text he took :
' Yea, after slaughter made at Ai,
When Joshua's three thousand fled,
Achan the thief they made to die—
They stoned him in this hollow here—
They burned him with his children dear ;
Among them flung his ingot red
And scarlet robe of Babylon :
Meet end for Carmi's wicked son
Because of whom they failed at Ai :
'Twas meet the trespasser should die ;
Yea, verily.'—His visage took
The tone of that uncanny nook.

    To Rolfe here Derwent : ' Study him ;
Then weigh that most ungenial rule
Of Moses and the austere school
Which e'en our saint can make so grim—
At least while Achor feeds his eyes.'
' But here speaks Nature otherwise ? '
Asked Rolfe ; ' in region roundabout
She 's Calvinistic if devout
In all her aspect.'—
                Vine, o'ercast,
Estranged rode in thought's hid repast.
Clarel, receptive, saw and heard,
Learning, unlearning, word by word.

    Erelong the wilds condense the ill—
They hump it into that black Hill
Named from the Forty Days and Nights,
The Quarantania's sum of blights.
Up from the gorge it grows, it grows :
Height sheer, sheer depth, and death's repose.
Sunk in the gulf the wave disowns,
Stranded lay ancient torrent-stones.

These Mortmain marks : ' Ah, from your deep
Turn ye, appeal ye to the steep ?
But that looks off, and everywhere
Descries but worlds more waste, more bare.'

      Flanked by the crag and glen they go.
Ahead, erelong in greeting show
The mounts of Moab, o'er the vale
Of Jordan opening into view,
With cloud-born shadows sweeping thro'.
      The Swede, intent : ' Lo, how they trail
The mortcloths in the funeral
Of gods ! '
            Although he naught confessed,
In Derwent, marking there the scene,
What interference was expressed
As of harsh grit in oiled machine—
Disrelish grating interest :
Howbeit, this he tried to screen.
' Pisgah ! ' cried Rolfe, and pointed him.
    ' Peor, too—ay, long Abarim
The ridge.   Well, well : for thee I sigh,
Poor Moses.   Saving Jericho
And her famed palms in Memphian row,
No cheerful landscape met thine eye ;
Unless indeed (yon Pisgah 's high)
Was caught, beyond each mount and plain,
The blue, blue Mediterranean.'
      ' And might he then for Egypt sigh ? '
Here prompted Rolfe ; but no reply ;
And Rolfe went on : ' Balboa's ken
Roved in fine sweep from Darien :
The woods and waves in tropic meeting,
Bright capes advancing, bays retreating—
Green land, blue sea in charm competing ! '

Meantime, with slant reverted eyes
Vine marked the Crag of Agonies.
Exceeding high (as Matthew saith)
It shows from skirt of that wild path
Bare as an iceberg seamed by rain
Toppling awash in foggy main
Off Labrador.   Grottoes Vine viewed
Upon the flank—or cells or tombs—
Void as the iceberg's catacombs
Of frost.   He starts.   A form endued
With living guise, from ledges dim
Leans as if looking down toward him.
Not pointing out the thing he saw
Vine watched it, but it showed no claw
Of hostile purpose ; tho' indeed
Robbers and outlaws armed have dwelt
Vigilant by those caves where knelt
Of old the hermits of the creed.

Beyond, they win a storied fount
Which underneath the higher mount
Gurgles, clay-white, and downward sets
Toward Jericho in rivulets,
Which—much like children whose small mirth
Not funerals can stay—through dearth
Run babbling.   One old humpbacked tree,
Sad grandam whom no season charms,
Droops o'er the spring her withered arms ;
And stones as in a ruin laid,
Like penitential benches be
Where silent thickets fling a shade
And gather dust.   Here halting, here
Awhile they rest and try the cheer.

XV

THE FOUNTAIN

It brake, it brake how long ago,
That morn which saw thy marvel done,
Elisha—healing of the spring !
A good deed lives, the doer low :
See how the waters eager run
With bounty which they chiming bring :
So out of Eden's bounds afar
Hymned Pison through green Havilah !

But ill those words in tone impart
The simple feelings in the heart
Of Nehemiah—full of the theme,
Standing beside the marge, with cup,
And pearls of water-beads adroop
Down thinnish beard of silvery gleam.

' Truly,' said Derwent, glad to note
That Achor found her antidote,
' Truly, the fount wells grateful here.'
Then to the student : ' For the rest,
The site is pleasant ; nor unblest
These thickets by their shade endear.'

Assent half vacant Clarel gave,
Watching that miracle the wave.

Said Rolfe, reclining by the rill,
' Needs life must end or soon or late :
Perchance set down it is in fate
That fail I must ere we fulfil

Our travel.   Should it happen true—
Attention, pray—I mend my will,
And name executors in you :
Bury me by the road, somewhere
Near spring or brook.   Palms plant me there,
And seats with backs to them, all stone :
In peace then go.   The years shall run,
And green my grave shall be, and play
The part of host to all that stray
In desert : water, shade, and rest
Their entertainment.   So I 'll win
Balm to my soul by each poor guest
That solaced leaves the Dead Man's Inn.
But charges, mind, yourselves defray—
Seeing I 've naught.'
                          Where thrown he lay,
Vine, sensitive, suffused did show,
Yet looked not up, but seemed to weigh
The nature of the heart whose trim
Of quaint good-fellowship could so
Strike on a chord long slack in him.

   But how may spirit quick and deep
A constancy unfreakish keep ?
A reed there shaken fitfully
He marks : ' Was 't this we came to see
In wilderness ? ' and rueful smiled.

   The meek one, otherwise beguiled,
Here chancing now the ass to note
Languidly munching straw and bran,
Drew nigh, and smoothed the roughened coat,
And gave her bread, the wheaten grain.
   Vine watches ; and his aspect knows
A flush of diffident humour : ' Nay,
Me too, me too let wait, I pray,
On our snubbed kin here ' ; and he rose.

Erelong, alert the escort show :
'Tis stirrups.   But the Swede moved not,
Aloof abiding in dark plot
Made by the deeper shadow : ' Go—
My horse lead ; but for me, I stay ;
Some bread—there, that small loaf will do :
It is my whim—my whim, I say ;
Mount, heed not me.'—' And how long, pray ? '
Asked Derwent, startled : ' eve draws on :
Ye would not tarry here alone ? '
    ' Thou man of God, nor desert here,
Nor Zin, nor Obi, yieldeth fear
If God but be—but be !   This waste—
Soon shall night fold the hemisphere ;
But safer then to lay me down,
Here, by yon evil Summit faced—
Safer than in the cut-throat town
Though on the church steps.   Go from me—
Begone !   To-morrow or next day
Jordan ye greet, then round ye sway
And win Lot's marge.   In sight ye 'll be :
I 'll intercept.   Ride on, go—nay,
Bewitched, why gape ye so at me ?
Shall man not take the natural way
With nature ?   Tut, fling me the cloak ! '
    Away, precipitate he broke,
The skull-cap glooming thro' the glade :
They paused, nor ventured to invade.

While so, not unconcerned, they stood,
The Druze said, ' Well, let be.   Why chafe ?
Nights here are mild ;   one 's pretty safe
When fearless.—Belex !   come, the road ! '

XVI

Look how a pine in luckless land
By fires autumnal overrun,
Abides a black extinguished brand
Gigantic—killed, not overthrown ;
And high upon the horny bough
Perches the bandit captain-crow
And caws unto his troop afar
Of foragers : much so, in scar
Of blastment, looms the Crusaders' Tower
On the waste verge of Jericho :
So the dun sheik in lawless power
Kings it aloft in sombre robe,
Lord of the tawny Arab mob
To which, upon the plains in view,
He shouts down his wild hullabaloo.

There on the tower, through eve's delay
The pilgrims tarry, till for boon,
Launched up from Nebo far away,
Balloon-like rose the nibbled moon—
Nibbled, being after full one day.
Intent they watched the planet's rise—
Familiar, tho' in strangest skies.
The ascending orb of furrowed gold,
Contracting, changed, and silvery rolled
In violet heaven. The desert brown,
Dipped in the dream of argent light,

Like iron plated, took a tone
Transmuting it ; and Ammon shone
In peaks of Paradise—so bright.
    They gazed. Rolfe brake upon the calm :
' O haunted place, O powerful charm !
Were now Elijah's chariot seen
(And yonder, read we writ aright,
He went up—over against this site)
Soaring in that deep heaven serene,
To me 'twould but in beauty rise ;
Nor hair-clad John would now surprise—
But Volney ! '
                ' Volney ? ' Derwent cried :
' Ah, yes ; he came to Jordan's side
A pilgrim deist from the Seine.'
    ' Ay, and Chateaubriand, he too,
The Catholic pilgrim, hither drew—
Here formed his purpose to assert
Religion in her just desert
Against the Red Caps of his time.
The book he wrote ; it dies away ;
But those Septemberists of crime
Enlarge in Vitriolists to-day.
Nor while we dwell upon this scene
Can one forget poor Lamartine—
A latter palmer. Oh, believe
When, his fine social dream to grieve,
Strode Fate, that realist how grim,
Displacing, deriding, hushing him,
Apt comment then might memory weave
In lesson from this waste.—That cry !
And would the jackal testify
From Moab ? '
             Derwent could but sway :
' Omit ye in citation, pray,

The healthy pilgrims of times old ?
Robust they were ; and cheery saw
Shrines, chapels, castles without flaw
Now gone. That river convent's fold,
By willows nigh the Pilgrims' Strand
Of Jordan, was a famous hold.
Prince Sigurd from the Norseman land,
Quitting his keel at Joppa, crossed
Hither, with Baldwin for his host,
And Templars for a guard. Perchance
Under these walls the train might prance
By Norman warder eyed.'
                    ' Maybe,'
Responded Vine ; ' but why disown
The Knight of the Leopard—even he,
Since hereabout that fount made moan,
Named Diamond of the Desert ? '—' Yes,'
Beamed Rolfe, divining him in clue ;
' Such shadows we, one need confess
That Scott's dreamed knight seems all but true
As men which history vouches. She—
Tasso's Armida, by Lot's sea,
Where that enchantress, with sweet look
Of kindliest human sympathy,
Such webs about Rinaldo wove
That all the hero he forsook—
Lost in the perfidies of love—
Armida—starts at fancy's bid
Not less than Rahab, lass which hid
The spies here in this Jericho.'

    A lull. Their thoughts, mute plunging, strayed
Like Arethusa under ground ;
While Clarel marked where slumber-bound
Lay Nehemiah in screening shade.

Erelong, in reappearing tide,
Rolfe, gazing forth on either side :
' How lifeless !　But the annual rout
At Easter here shall throng and shout,
Far populate the lonely plain
(Next day a solitude again),
All pressing unto Jordan's dew ;
While in the saddle of disdain
Skirr the Turk guards with fierce halloo,
Armed herdsmen of the drove.'　He ceased ;
And fell the silence unreleased
Till yet again did Rolfe round peer
Upon that moonlit land of fear :
　　　' Man sprang from deserts : at the touch
Of grief or trial overmuch
On deserts he falls back at need ;
Yes, 'tis the bare abandoned home
Recalleth then.　See how the Swede,
Like any rustic crazy Tom,
Bursting through every code and ward
Of civilisation, masque and fraud,
Takes the wild plunge.　Who so secure,
Except his clay be sodden loam,
As never to dream the day may come
When *he* may take it, foul or pure ?
What in these turns of mortal tides—
What any fellow-creature bides,
May hap to any.'
　　　　　　　' Pardon, pray,'
Cried Derwent—' but 'twill quick away :
Yon moon in pearl-cloud : look, her face
Peers like a bride's from webs of lace.'
They gazed until it faded there :
When Rolfe with a discouraged air
Sat as rebuked.　In winning strain,

As 'twere in penitence urbane,
Here Derwent, ' Come, we wait thee now.'
   ' No matter,' Rolfe said ; ' let it go.
My earnestness myself decry ;
But as heaven made me, so am I.'
   ' You spake of Mortmain,' breathed Vine low.
As embers, not yet cold, will catch
Quick at the touch of smallest match,
Here Rolfe : ' In gusts of lonely pain
Beating upon the naked brain——'
   ' God help him, ay, poor realist ! '
So Derwent, and that theme dismissed.

When Ashtaroth her zenith won,
Sleep drugged them and the winds made moan.

XVII

IN MID-WATCH

Disturbed by topics canvassed late,
Clarel, from dreams of like debate,
Started, and heard strange muffled sounds,
Outgivings of wild mountain bounds.
He rose, stood gazing toward the height—
Bethinking him that thereaway
Behind it o'er the desert lay
The walls that sheltered Ruth that night—
When Rolfe drew near.   With motion slight,
Scarce conscious of the thing he did,
Partly aside the student slid ;
Then, quick as thought, would fain atone.
          Whence came that shrinking start unbid ?
But from desire to be alone ?
Or skim or sound him, was Rolfe one
Whom honest heart would care to shun ?
By spirit immature or dim
Was nothing to be learned from him ?
How frank seemed Rolfe.   Yet Vine could lure
Despite reserve which overture
Withstood—e'en Clarel's—late repealed,
Finding that heart a fountain sealed.

          But Rolfe : however it might be—
Whether in friendly fair advance
Checked by that start of dissonance,
Or whether rapt in revery

Beyond—apart he moved, and leant
Down peering from the battlement
Upon its shadow. Then and there
Clarel first noted in his air
A gleam of oneness more than Vine's—
The irrelation of a weed
Detached from vast Sargossa's mead,
And drifting where the clear sea shines.

But Clarel turned him ; and anew
His thoughts regained their prior clue ;
When lo, a fog, and all was changed.
Crept vapours from the Sea of Salt,
Overspread the plain, nor there made halt,
But blurred the heaven.
　　　　　　　　As one estranged
Who watches, watches from the shore,
Till the white speck is seen no more,
The ship that bears his plighted maid,
Then turns and sighs as fears invade ;
See here the student, repossessed
By thoughts of Ruth, with eyes late pressed
Whither lay Salem, close and wynd—
The mist before him, mist behind,
While intercepting memories ran
Of chant and bier Armenian.

XVIII

THE SYRIAN MONK

At early hour with Rolfe and Vine
Clarel ascends a minor height ;
They overtake in lone recline
A strange wayfarer of the night
Who, 'twixt the small hour and the gray,
With cruse and scrip replenished late
In Jericho at the wattled gate,
Had started on the upland way :
A young strange man of aspect thin
From vigils which in fast begin.
Though, pinned together with the thorn,
His robe was ragged all and worn—
Pure did he show as mountain-leaf
By brook, or coral washed in reef.
Contrasting with the bleached head-dress
His skin revealed such swarthiness,
And in the contour clear and grace,
So all unworldly was the face,
He looked a later Baptist John.
They start ; surprise perforce they own :
Much like Da Gama's men, may be,
When sudden on their prow at sea
Lit the strange bird from shores unknown.

　　　Although at first from words he shrunk,
He was, they knew, a Syrian monk,
They so prevailed with him and pressed,
He longer lingered at request.

They won him over in the end
To tell his story and unbend.

He told how that for forty days,
Not yet elapsed, he dwelt in ways
Of yonder Quarantanian height,
A true recluse, an anchorite ;
And only came at whiles below,
And ever in the calm of night,
To beg for scraps in Jericho.
'Twas sin, he said, that drove him out
Into the desert—sin of doubt.
Even he it was upon the mount
By chance perceived, untold, by Vine,
From Achor's brink. He gave account
Of much besides ; his lonely mine
Of deep illusion ; how the night,
The first, was spent upon the height,
And way he climbed :
                              ' Up cliff, up crag—
Cleft crag and cliff which still retard,
Goat-like I scrambled where stones lag
Poised on the brinks by thunder marred.
A ledge I reached which midway hung
Where a hut-oratory clung—
Rude stones massed up, with cave-like door,
Eremite work of days of yore.
White bones here lay, remains of feast
Dragged in by bird of prey or beast.
Hence gazed I on the wilds beneath,
Dengadda and the coasts of death.
But not a tremor felt I here :
It was upon the summit fear
First fell ; there first I saw this world ;
And scarce man's place it seemed to be ;

The mazed Gehennas so were curled
As worm-tracks under bark of tree.
I ween not if to ye 'tis known—
Since few do know the crag aright,
Years left unvisited and lone—
That a wrecked chapel marks the site
Where tempter and the tempted stood
Of old. I sat me down to brood
Within that ruin ; and—my heart
Unwaveringly to set apart
In meditation upon Him
Who here endured the evil whim
Of Satan—steadfast, steadfast down
Mine eyes fixed on a flinty stone
Which lay there at my feet. But thought
Would wander. Then the stone I caught,
Convulsed it in my hand till blood
Oozed from these nails. Then came and stood
The Saviour there—the Imp and He :
Fair showed the Fiend—foul enemy ;
But, ah, the Other pale and dim :
I saw but as the shade of Him.
That passed. Again I was alone—
Alone—ah, no—not long alone :
As glides into dead grass the snake
Lean rustling from the bedded brake,
A spirit entered me. 'Twas he,
The tempter, in return ; but *me*
He tempted now. He mocked : " Why strife ?
Dost hunger for the bread of life ?
Thou lackest faith : faith would be fed ;
True faith could turn that stone to bread,
That stone thou hold'st."—Mute then my face
I lifted to the starry space ;
But the great heaven it burned so bright,

It cowed me, and back fell my sight.
Then he : " Is yon the Father's home ?
And thou His child cast out to night ?
'Tis bravely lighted, yonder dome."—
" Part speak'st thou true : yea, He is there."—
" Yea, yea, and He is everywhere—
Now and for aye, Evil and He."—
" Is there no good ? "—" Ill to fulfil
Needful is good : good salts the ill."—
" He 's just."—" Goodness is justice. See,
Through all the pirate-spider's snare
Of silken arcs of gossamer,
'Tis delicate geometry :
Adorest the artificer ? "—
No answer knew I, save this way :
" Faith bideth."—" Noon, and wait for day ?
The sand 's half run ! Eternal, He :
But aye with a futurity
Which not exceeds His past. Agree,
Full time has lapsed. What ages hoar,
What period fix, when faith no more,
If unfulfilled, shall fool ? "—I sat ;
Sore quivered I to answer that,
Yet answered naught ; but lowly said—
" And death ? "—" Why beat the bush in thee ?
It is the cunningest mystery :
Alive thou know'st not death ; and, dead,
Death thou 'lt not know."—" The grave will test ;
But He, He *is*, though doubt attend ;
Peace will He give ere come the end."—
" Ha, *thou* at peace ?   Nay, peace were best—
Could the unselfish yearner rest !
At peace to be, here, here on earth,
Where peace, heart-peace, how few may claim,
And each pure nature pines in dearth—

Fie, fie, thy soul might well take shame."—
There sunk my heart—he spake so true
In that. O God (I prayed), come through
The cloud ; hard task Thou settest man
To know Thee ; take me back again
To nothing, or make clear my view !—
Then stole the whisper intermitting ;
Like tenon into mortice fitting
It slipped into the frame of me :
" Content thee : in conclusion caught
Thou 'lt find how thought's extremes agree—
The forethought clinched by afterthought,
The firstling by finality."—
There close fell, and therewith the stone
Dropped from my hand.—His will be done ! '
      And skyward patient he appealed,
Raising his eyes, and so revealed
First to the pilgrims' waiting view
Their virginal violet of hue.

      Rolfe spake : ' Surely, not all we 've heard :
Peace—solace—was in end conferred ? '—
His head but fell.   He rose in haste,
The rough hair-girdle tighter drew
About the hollow of the waist,
Departing with a mild adieu.

      They sat in silence.   Rolfe at last :
' And this but ecstasy of fast ?
Construe then Jonah in despair.'—
The student turned, awaiting Vine ;
Who answered nothing, plaiting there
A weed from neighbouring ground uptorn,
Plant common enough in Palestine,
And by the peasants named Christ's Thorn.

XIX

AN APOSTATE

'BARQUE, Easter barque, with happier freight
Than Spanish spoil of Inca plate ;
Which vernal glidest from the strand
Of statues poised like angels fair ;
On March morn sailest—starting, fanned
Auspicious by Sardinian air ;
And carriest boughs thro' Calpe's gate
To Norman ports and Belgian land,
That the Green Sunday, even there,
No substituted leaf may wear,
Holly or willow's lither wand,
But sprays of Christ's canonic tree,
Rome's Palma-Christi by decree,
The Date Palm ; ah, in bounty launch,
Thou blessed Easter barque, to me
Hither one consecrated branch ! '

So Rolfe in burst, and turned toward Vine ;
But he the thorn-wreath still did twine.
Rolfe watched him busy there and dumb,
Then cried : ' Did gardens favour it,
How would I match thee here, and sit
Wreathing Christ's flower, chrysanthemum.'

Erelong the Syrian they view
In slow ascent, and also two
Between him and the peak—one wight,
An Arab with a pouch, nor light,

A desert Friday to the one
Who went before him, coming down,
Shagged Crusoe, by the mountain spur.
This last, when he the votary meets
Sad climbing slow, him loudly greets,
Stopping with questions which refer
In some way to the crag amort—
The crag, since thitherward his hand
Frequent he waves, as with demand
For some exact and clear report
Touching the place of his retreat
Aloft.   As seemed, in neutral plight
Submiss responds the anchorite,
The wallet dropped beside his feet.
These part.   Master and man now ply
Yet down the slope ; and he in van—
Round-shouldered, and tho' gray yet spry—
A hammer swung.

     I 've met that man
Elsewhere (thought Clarel)—he whose cry
And gibe came up from the dung-gate
In hollow, when we scarce did wait
His nearer speech and wagging head,
The saint and I.—But naught he said
Hereof.

    The stranger closer drew ;
And Rolfe breathed ' This now is a Jew—
German, I deem—but readvised—
An Israelite, say, Hegelised—
Convert to science, for but see
The hammer : yes, geology.'
As now the other's random sight
On Clarel mute and Vine is thrown,
He misinterprets their grave plight ;
And, with a banter in the tone,
Amused he cries : ' Now, now, yon height—

Come, let it not alarm : a mount
Whereof I 've taken strict account
(Its first geologist, believe),
And, if my eyes do not deceive,
'Tis Jura limestone, every spur ;
Yes, and tho' signs the rocks imprint
Which of Plutonic action hint,
No track is found, I plump aver,
Of Pluto's footings—Lucifer.'

    The punning mock and manner stirred
Repugnance in fastidious Vine ;
But Rolfe, who tolerantly heard,
Parleyed, and won him to define
At large his rovings on the height.
    The yester-afternoon and night
He 'd spent there, sleeping in a cave—
Part for adventure, part to spite
The superstition, and outbrave.
'Twas a severe ascent, he said ;
In bits a ladder of steep stone
With toe-holes cut, and worn, each one
By eremites long centuries dead.
And of his cullings too, he told :
His henchman here, the Arab wight,
Bare solid texts from Bible old—
True Rock of Ages, he averred.
To read before a learned board,
When home regained should meet his sight,
A monograph he would indite—
The theme, that crag.
              He went his way
To win the tower.   Little they say ;
But Clarel started at the view
Which showed opposed the anchorite
Ascetical and—such a Jew.

XX

UNDER THE MOUNTAIN

FROM Ur of the Chaldees roved the man—
Priest, shepherd, prince, and pioneer—
Swart Bedouin in time's dusky van ;
Even he which first, with mind austere,
Arrived in solitary tone
To think of God as One—alone ;
The first which brake with hearth and home
For conscience' sake ; whom piety ruled,
Prosperity blest, longevity schooled,
And time in fullness brought to Mamre's tomb
Arch founder of the solid base of Christendom.
    Even this. For why disown the debt
When vouchers be ? Yet, yet and yet
Our saving salt of grace is due
All to the East—nor least the Jew.
    Perverse, if stigma then survive,
Elsewhere let such in satire thrive—
Not here. Quite other end is won
In picturing Margoth, fallen son
Of Judah. Him may Gabriel mend.

    Little for love, or to unbend,
But swayed by tidings, hard to sift,
Of robbers by the river-drift
In force recruited ; they suspend
Their going hence to Jordan's trees.
Released from travel, in good hour
Nehemiah dozed within the tower.

Uplands they range, and woo the breeze
Where crumbled aqueducts and mounds
Override long slopes and terraces,
And shattered pottery abounds—
Or such would seem, yet may but be
The shards of tile-like brick dispersed
Binding the wall or bulwark erst,
Such as in Kent still serve that end
In Richborough castle by the sea—
A Roman hold. What breadth of doom
As of the worlds in strata penned—
So cosmic seems the wreck of Rome.
　　Not wholly proof to natural sway
Of serious hearts and manners mild,
Uncouthly Margoth shared the way.
He controverted all the wild,
And in especial, Sodom's strand
Of marl and clinker : ' Sirs, heed me :
This total tract,' and Esau's hand
He waved ; ' the plain—the vale—Lot's sea—
It needs we scientists remand
Back from old theologic myth
To geologic hammers. Pray,
Let me but give ye here the pith :
As the Phlegræan fields no more
Befool men as the spookish shore
Where Jove felled giants, but are known—
The Solfatara and each cone
Volcanic—to be but on a par
With all things natural ; even so
Siddim shall likewise be set far
From fable.'
　　　　　　Part overhearing this,
Derwent, in rear with Rolfe : ' Old clo' !
We 've heard all that, and long ago :

Conceit of vacant emphasis :
Well, well ! '—Here archly, Rolfe : ' But
    own,
How graceful your concession—won
A score or two of years gone by.
Nor less therefrom at need ye 'll fly,
Allow. Scarce easy 'tis to hit
Each slippery turn of cleric wit.'
Derwent but laughed ; then said—' But *he* :
Intelligence veneers his mien
Though rude : unprofitably keen :
Sterile, and with sterility
Self-satisfied.' ' But this is odd !
Not often do we hear you rail :
The gown it seems does yet avail,
Since from the sleeve you draw the rod.
But look, they lounge.'

                  Yes, all recline,
And on the site where havoc clove
The last late palm of royal line,
Sad Montezuma of the grove.
The mountain of the Imp they see
Scowl at the freedom which they take
Relaxed beneath his very lee.
    The bread of wisdom here to break,
Margoth holds forth : the gossip tells
Of things the prophets left unsaid—
With master-key unlocks the spells
And mysteries of the world unmade ;
Then mentions Salem : ' Stale is she !
Lay flat the walls, let in the air,
That folk no more may sicken there !
Wake up the dead ; and let there be
Rails, wires, from Olivet to the sea,
With station in Gethsemane.'

The priest here flushed. Rolfe rose : and,
 ' How—
You go too far ! ' ' A long Dutch mile
Behind the genius of our time.'
' Explain that, pray.' ' And don't you know ?
Malbrino's helmet is sublime—
The barber's basin may be vile :
Whether this basin is that helm
To vast debate has given rise—
Question profound for blinking eyes ;
But common sense throughout her realm
Has settled it.'
    There, like vain wight
His fine thing said, bidding friends good-night,
He, to explore a rift they see,
Parted, bequeathing, as might be,
A glance which said—Again ye 'll pine
Left to yourselves here in decline,
Missing my brave vitality !

XXI

THE PRIEST AND ROLFE

DERWENT fetched breath : ' A healthy man :
His lungs are of the soundest leather.'
' Health 's insolence in a Saurian,'
Said Rolfe.   With that they fell together
Probing the purport of the Jew
In last ambiguous words he threw.
But Derwent, and in lenient way,
Explained it.
          ' Let him have his say,'
Cried Rolfe ; ' for one, I spare defiance
With such a kangaroo of science.'
     ' Yes ; qualify though,' Derwent said,
' For science has her eagles too.'
     Here musefully Rolfe hung the head ;
Then lifted : ' Eagles ? ay ; but few.
And search we in their aeries lone
What find we, pray ? perchance, a bone.'
     ' A very cheerful point of view ! '
' 'Tis as one takes it.   Not unknown
That even in Physics much late lore
But drudges after Plato's theme ;
Or supplements—but little more—
Some Hindoo's speculative dream
Of thousand years ago.   And, own,
Darwin is but his grandsire's son.'
     ' But Newton and his gravitation ! '
' Think you that system's strong persuasion

Is founded beyond shock ?   O'ermuch
'Twould seem for man, a clod, to clutch
God's secret so, and on a slate
Cipher all out, and formulate
The universe.'   ' You Pyrrhonist !
Why, now, perhaps you do not see—
Your mind has taken such a twist—
The claims of stellar chemistry.'
    ' What 's that ? '   ' No matter.   Time
      runs on
And much that 's useful, grant, is won.'
    ' Yes ; but more 's claimed.   Now first they
      tell
The human mind is free to range.
Enlargement—ay ; but where 's the change ?
We 're yet within the citadel—
May rove in bounds, and study out
The insuperable towers about.'
    ' Come ; but there 's many a merry man :
How long since these sad times began ? '
    That steadied Rolfe : ' Where 's no annoy
I too perchance can take a joy—
Yet scarce in solitude of thought :
Together cymbals need be brought
Ere mirth is made.   The wight alone
Who laughs, is deemed a witless one.
And why ?   But that we 'll leave unsought.'
    ' By all means !—O ye frolic shapes :
Thou Dancing Faun, thou Faun with Grapes !
What think ye of them ? tell us, pray.'
    ' Fine mellow marbles.'
                    ' But their hint ? '
' A mine as deep as rich the mint
Of cordial joy in Nature's sway
Shared somewhere by anterior clay

When life was innocent and free :
Methinks 'tis this they hint to me.'
    He paused, as one who makes review
Of gala days ; then—warmly too—
' Whither hast fled, thou deity
So genial ? In thy last and best,
Best avatar—so ripe in form—
Pure as the sleet—as roses warm—
Our earth's unmerited fair guest—
A god with peasants went abreast :
Man clasped a deity's offered hand ;
And woman, ministrant, was then
How true, even in a Magdalen.
Him following through the wilding flowers
By lake and hill, or glad detained
In Cana—ever out of doors—
Ere yet the disenchantment gained
What dream they knew, that primal band
Of gipsy Christians ! But it died ;
Back rolled the world's effacing tide :
The " *world* "—by Him denounced, defined—
Him first—set off and countersigned,
Once and for all, as opposite
To honest children of the light.
But worse came—creeds, wars, stakes. Oh, men
Made earth inhuman ; yes, a den
Worse for Christ's coming, since His love
(Perverted) did but venom prove.
In part that 's passed. But what remains
After fierce seethings ? golden grains ?
Nay, dubious dregs : be frank, and own.
Opinion eats ; all crumbles down :
Where stretched an isthmus, rolls a strait :
Cut off, cut off ! Canst feel elate
While all the depths of Being moan,

Though luminous on every hand,
The breadths of shallow knowledge more expand ?
Much as a lightship keeper pines
Mid shoals immense, where dreary shines
His lamp, we toss beneath the ray
Of Science' beacon. This to trim
Is now man's barren office.—Nay,'
Starting abrupt, ' this earnest way
I hate. Let doubt alone ; best skim,
Not dive.'
        ' No, no,' cried Derwent gay,
Who late, upon acquaintance more,
Took no mislike to Rolfe at core,
And fain would make his knell a chime—
Being pledged to hold the palmy time
Of hope—at least, not to admit
That serious check might come to it :
' No, sun doubt's root—'twill fade, 'twill fade !
And for thy picture of the Prime,
Green Christianity in glade—
Why, let it pass ; 'tis good, in sooth :
Who summons poets to the truth ? '

   How Vine sidelong regarded him
As 'twere in envy of his gift
For light disposings : so to skim !
   Clarel surmised the expression's drift,
Thereby anew was led to sift
Good Derwent's mind. For Rolfe's discourse—
Prior recoil from Margoth's jeer
Was less than startled shying here
At earnest comment's random force.
He shrunk ; but owned 'twas weakness mere.
Himself he chid : No more for me
The petty half-antipathy :

This pressure it need be endured :
Weakness to strength must get inured ;
And Rolfe is sterling, though not less
At variance with that parlour-strain
Which counts each thought that borders pain
A social treason.   Sterling—yes,
Despite illogical wild range
Of brain and heart's impulsive counterchange.

XXII

As by the wood drifts thistle-down
And settles on soft mosses fair,
Stillness was wafted, dropped and sown ;
Which stillness Vine, with timorous air
Of virgin tact, thus brake upon,
Nor with chance hint : ' One can't forbear
Thinking that Margoth is—a *Jew.*'
      Hereat, as for reponse, they view
The priest.
            ' And, well, why me ? ' he cried ;
' With one consent why turn to *me* ?
Am I professional ?   Nay, free !
I grant that here by Judah's side
Queerly it jars with frame implied
To list this geologic Jew,
His way Jehovah's world construe :
In Gentile 'twould not seem so odd.
But here may preconceptions thrall ?
Be many Hebrews we recall
Whose contrast with the breastplate bright
Of Aaron flushed in altar-light,
And Horeb's Moses, rock and rod,
Or closeted alone with God,
Quite equals Margoth's in its way :
At home we meet them every day.
The Houndsditch clothesman scarce would seem
Akin to seers.   For one, I deem

Jew banker, merchant, statesman—these,
With artist, actress known to fame,
All strenuous in each Gentile aim,
Are Nature's off-hand witnesses
There 's nothing mystic in her reign :
Your Jew 's like wheat from Pharaoh's tomb :
Sow it in England, what will come ?
The weird old seed yields market grain.'

    Pleased by his wit while some recline,
A smile uncertain lighted Vine,
But died away.

              ' Jews share the change,'
Derwent proceeded : ' Range, they range—
In liberal sciences they roam ;
They 're leavened, and it works, believe ;
Signs are, and such as scarce deceive.
From Holland, that historic home
Of erudite Israel, many a tome
Talmudic shipped is over sea
For antiquarian rubbish.'

                 ' Rest ! '
Cried Rolfe ; ' e'en that indeed may be,
Nor less the Jew keep fealty
To ancient rites.   Aaron's gemmed vest
Will long outlive Genevan cloth—
Nothing in Time's old camphor-chest
So little subject to the moth.
But Rabbis have their troublers too.
Nay, if thro' dusty stalls we look,
Haply we disinter to view
More than one bold freethinking Jew
That in his day with vigour shook
Faith's leaning tower.'

           ' Which stood the throe,'
Here Derwent in appendix : ' look,

Faith's leaning tower was founded so :
Faith leaned from the beginning ; yes,
If slant, she holds her steadfastness.'
    ' May be ' ; and paused : ' but wherefore
       clog ?—
Uriel Acosta, he was one
Who troubled much the synagogue—
Recanted then, and dropped undone :
A suicide. There 's Heine, too
(In lineage crossed by blood of Jew),
Pale jester, to whom life was yet
A tragic farce ; whose wild death-rattle,
In which all voids and hollows met,
Desperately maintained the battle
Betwixt the dirge and castanet.
But him leave to his Paris stone
And rail, and friendly wreath thereon.
Recall those Hebrews, which of old
Sharing some doubts we moderns rue,
Would fain Eclectic comfort fold
By grafting slips from Plato's palm
On Moses' melancholy yew :
But did they sprout ? So *we* seek balm
By kindred graftings. Is that true ? '
    ' Why ask ? But see : there lived a Jew—
No Alexandrine Greekish one—
You know him—Moses Mendelssohn.'
    ' Is 't him you cite ? True spirit staid,
He, though his honest heart was scourged
By doubt Judaic, never laid
His burden at Christ's door ; he urged—
" Admit the mounting flames enfold
My basement ; wisely shall my feet
The attic win, for safe retreat ? " '
    ' And *he* said that ? Poor man, he 's cold.

But was not this that Mendelssohn
Whose Hebrew kinswoman's Hebrew son,
Baptized to Christian, worthily won
The good name of Neander so ? '
   ' If that link were, well might one urge
From such example, thy strange flow,
Conviction ! Breaking habit's tether,
Sincerest minds will yet diverge
Like chance clouds scattered by mere weather ;
Nor less at one point still they meet :
The selfhood keep they pure and sweet.'

   ' But Margoth,' in reminder here
Breathed Vine, as if while yet the ray
Lit Rolfe, to try his further cheer :
' But Margoth ! '
                ' He, poor sheep astray,
The Levitic cipher quite erased,
On what vile pig-weed hath he grazed.
Not his Spinoza's starry brow
(A non-conformer, ye 'll allow),
A lion in brain, in life a lamb,
Sinless recluse of Amsterdam ;
Who, in the obscure and humble lane,
Such strangers seemed to entertain
As sat by tent beneath the tree
On Mamre's plain—mysterious three,
The informing guests of Abraham.
But no, it had but ill beseemed
If God's own angels so could list
To visit one, Pan's Atheist.
That high intelligence but dreamed—
Above delusion's vulgar plain
Deluded still. The erring twain,
Spinoza and poor Margoth here,

Both Jews, which in dissent do vary :
In these what parted poles appear—
The blind man and the visionary.'
 ' And whose the eye that sees aright,
If any ? ' Clarel eager asked.
Aside Rolfe turned as overtasked ;
And none responded.   'Twas like night
Descending from the seats of light,
Or seeming thence to fall.   But here
Sedate a kindly tempered look
Private and confidential spoke
From Derwent's eyes, Clarel to cheer :
Take heart ; something to fit thy youth
Instil I may, some saving truth—
Not best just now to volunteer.
  Thought Clarel : Pray, and what wouldst
   prove ?
Thy faith an over-easy glove.

  Meanwhile Vine had relapsed.   They saw
In silence the heart's shadow draw—
Rich shadow, such as gardens keep
In bower aside, where glow-worms peep
In evening over the virgin bed
Where dark-green periwinkles sleep—
Their bud the Violet of the Dead.

XXIII

BY THE JORDAN

On the third morn, a misty one,
Equipped they sally for the wave
Of Jordan. With his escort brown
The Israelite attendance gave
For that one day and night alone.
Slung by a cord from saddle-bow,
Is it the mace of Ivanhoe ?
　　　Rolfe views, and comments : 'Note, I pray,'
He said to Derwent on the way,
'Yon knightly hammer. 'Tis with that
He stuns, and would exterminate
Your creeds as dragons.'
　　　　　　　With light fire
Of wit, the priest rejoinder threw ;
But turned to look at Nehemiah :
The labouring ass with much ado
Of swerving neck would, at the sight
Of bramble-tops, snatch for a bite ;
And though it bred him joltings ill—
In patience that did never tire,
Her rider let her have her will.
　　　The apostate, ready with his sneer :
'Yes, you had better—'tis a *she*.'
　　　To Rolfe said Derwent : 'There, you see :
It is these infidels that jeer
At everything.'

               The Jew withheld
His mare, and let Nehemiah pass :
' Who is this Balaam on the ass ? '
But none his wonderment dispelled.

     Now skies distil a vaporous rain ;
So looked the sunken slimy plain—
Such semblance of the vacuum shared,
As 'twere the quaking sea-bed bared
By the Caracas.　All was still :
So much the more their bosoms thrill
With dream of some withdrawn vast surge
Its timed return about to urge
And whelm them.
               But a cry they hear :
The steed of Mortmain, led in rear,
Broke loose and ran.　' Horse too run mad ? '
Cried Derwent ; ' shares his rider's mind—
His rider late ? shun both their kind ?
Poor Swede !　But where was it he said
We should rejoin ? '　' 'Tis by Lot's sea,
Remember.　And pray heaven it be !—
Look, the steed 's caught.'
               Suspicious ground
They skirt, with ugly bushes crowned ;
And thereinto, against surprise,
The vigilant Spahi throws his eyes :
To take of distant chance a bond,
Djalea looks forward, and beyond,
    At this, some riders feel that awe　·
Which comes of sense of absent law,
And irreligious human kind,
Relapsed, remanded, reassigned
To chaos and brute passions blind.
    But is it Jordan, Jordan dear,

That doth that evil bound define
Which borders on the barbarous sphere—
Jordan, even Jordan, stream divine ?
In Clarel ran such revery here.

Belex his flint adjusts and rights,
Sharp speaks unto his Bethlehemites ;
Then, signalled by Djalea, through air
Surveys the further ridges bare.
Foreshortened 'gainst a long-sloped height
Beyond the wave whose wash of foam
Beats to the base of Moab home,
Seven furious horsemen fling their flight
Like eagles when they launching rush
To snatch the prey that hies to bush.
Dwarfed so these look, while yet afar
Descried.   But trusting in their star,
Onward a space the party push ;
But halt is called ; the Druze rides on,
Bids Belex stand, and goes alone.

Now, for the nonce, those speeders sink
Viewless behind the arborous brink.
Thereto the staid one rides—peers in—
Then waves a hand.   They gain his side,
Meeting the river's rapid tide
Here sluicing through embowered ravine
Such as of yore was Midian's screen
For rites impure.   Facing, and near,
Across the waves which intervene,
In shade the robbers reappear :
Swart, sinuous men on silvery steeds—
Abreast, save where the copse impedes.
At halt, and mute, and in the van
Confronting them, with lengthy gun
Athwart the knee, and hand thereon,

Djalea waits. The mare and man
Show like a stone equestrian
Set up for homage. Over there
'Twas hard for mounted men to move
Among the thickets interwove,
Which dipped the stream and made a snare.
But, undeterred, the riders press
This way and that among the branches,
Picking them lanes through each recess,
Till backward on their settling haunches
The steeds withstand the slippery slope,
While yet their outflung forefeet grope ;
Then, like sword-push that ends in lunge,
The slide becomes a weltering plunge :
The willows drip, the banks resound ;
They halloo, and with spray are crowned.
The torrent, swelled by Lebanon rains,
The spirited horses bravely stem,
Snorting, half-blinded by their manes,
Nor let the current master them.
As the rope-dancer on the hair
Poises the long slim pole in air ;
Twirling their slender spears in pride,
Each horseman in imperilled seat
Blends skill and grace with courage meet.
      Soon as they win the hither side,
Like quicksilver to beach they glide,
Dismounting, and essay the steep,
The horses led by slackened rein :
Slippery foothold ill they keep.
To help a grim one of the band
Good Nehemiah with mickle strain
Down reaches a decrepit hand :
The sheik ignores it—bandit dun,
Foremost in stride as first in rank—

Rejects it, and the knoll is won.
Challengingly he stares around,
Then stakes his spear upon the bank
As one reclaiming rightful ground.
Like otters when to land they go,
Riders and steeds how sleekly show.

The first inquiring look they trace
Is gun by gun, as face by face :
Salute they yield, for arms they view
Inspire respect sincere and true.

Meantime, while in their bearing shows
The thought which still their life attends,
And habit of encountering foes—
The thought that strangers scarce are friends—
What think the horses ? Zar must needs
Be sociable ; the robber steeds
She whinnies to ; even fain would sway
Neck across neck in lovesome way.
Great Solomon, of rakish strain,
Trumpets—would be Don John again.

The sheik, without a moment's doubt,
Djalea for captain singles out ;
And, after parley brief, would fain
Handle that pistol of the guide,
The new revolver at his side.
The Druze assents, nor shows surprise.
Barrel, cap, screw, the Arab tries ;
And ah, the contrast needs he own :
Alack, for his poor lance and gun,
Though heirlooms both : the piece in stock
Half honeycombed, with cumbrous lock ;
The spear like some crusader's pole
Dropped long ago when death-damps stole
Over the knight in Richard's host,
Then left to warp by Acre lost :

Dry rib of lance.   But turning now
Upon his sweetheart, he was cheered.
Her eye he met, the violet-glow,
Peaked ear, the mane's redundant flow ;
It heartened him, and round he veered ;
Elate he shot a brigand glare :
I, Ishmael, have my desert mare !

Elicited by contact's touch,
Tyrannous spleen vexed Belex much,
Misliking in poor tribe to mark
Freedom unawed and nature's spark.
With tutoring glance, a tempered fire,
The Druze repressed the illiberal ire.
        The silvered saint came gently near,
Meekly intrepid, tract in hand,
And reached it with a heart sincere
Unto the sheik, whose fingers spanned
The shrewd revolver, loath to let
That coveted bauble go as yet.
' Nay,' breathed the Druze, and gently here :
' The print he likes not ; let him be ;
Pray now, he deems it sorcery.'
They drew him back.   In rufflement
The sheik threw round a questioning eye ;
Djalea explained, and drew more nigh,
Recalling him to old content ;
Regained the weapon ; and, from stores
Kept for such need, wary he pours
A dole of powder.
                So they part—
Recrossing Jordan, horse and gun,
With warrior cry and brandished dart,
Where, in the years whose goal is won,
The halcyon Teacher waded in with John.

XXIV

THE RIVER-RITE

AND do the clear sands pure and cold
At last each virgin elf enfold ?
Under what drift of silvery spar
Sleeps now thy servant, Holy Rood,
Which in the age of brotherhood
Approaching here Bethabara
By wilds the verse depicted late,
Of Jordan caught a fortunate
Fair twinkle starry under trees ;
And, with his crossed palms heartward pressed,
Bowed him, or dropped on reverent knees,
Warbling that hymn of beauty blest—
The *Ave maris stella* ?—Lo,
The mound of him do field-mice know ?
Nor less the rite, a rule serene,
Appropriate in tender grace,
Became the custom of the place
With each devouter Frank.

                              A truce
Here following the din profuse
Of Moab's swimming robbers keen,
Rolfe, late enamoured of the spell
Of rituals olden, thought it well
To observe the Latin usage : ' Look,'
Showing a small convenient book
In vellum bound ; embossed thereon,
'Tween angels with a rosy crown,
Viols, Cecilia on a throne :

' Thanks, friar Benignus Muscatel ;
Thy gift I prize, given me in cell
Of St. John's convent.—Comrades, come !
If heaven delight in spirits glad,
And men were all for brothers made,
Grudge not, beseech, to joy with Rome ' ;
And launched the hymn.   Quick to rejoice,
The liberal priest lent tenor voice ;
And marking them in cheery bloom
On turf inviting, even Vine,
Ravished from his reserve supine,
Drew near and overlooked the page—
All self-surprised he overlooked,
Joining his note impulsively ;
Yet, flushing, seemed as scarce he brooked
This joy.   Was joy a novelty ?
Fraternal thus, the group engage—
While now the sun, obscured before,
Illumed for time the wooded shore—
In tribute to the beach and tide.
      The triple voices blending glide,
Assimilating more and more,
Till in the last ascriptive line
Which thrones the Father, lauds the Son,
Came concord full, completion fine—
Rapport of souls in harmony of tone.

      Meantime Nehemiah, eager bent,
Instinctive caught the sentiment ;
But checked himself ; and, in mixed mood,
Uncertain or relapsing stood,
Till ere the singers cease to thrill,
His joy is stayed.   How cometh this ?
True feeling, steadfast faith are his,
While they at best do but fulfil

A transient, an æsthetic glow ;
Knew he at last—could he but know—
The rite was alien ? that no form
Approved was his, which here might warm
Meet channel for emotion's tide ?
Apart he went, scarce satisfied ;
But presently slipped down to where
The river ran, and tasting spare,
Not quaffing, sighed, ' As sugar sweet ! '
Though unsweet was it from the flow
Of turbid, troubled waters fleet.

Now Margoth—who had paced the strand
Gauging the level of the land,
Computing part the Jordan's fall
From Merom's spring, and therewithal
Had ended with a river-sip,
Which straight he spewed—here curled the lip
At hearing Nehemiah : The fool !
Fool meek and fulsome like to this—
Too old again to go to school—
Was never ! wonder who he is ;
I 'll ask himself.—' Who art thou, say ? '
' The chief of sinners.'—' Lack-a-day,
I think so too ' ; and moved away,
Low muttering in his ill content
At that so Christian bafflement ;
And hunted up his sumpter mule
Intent on lunch. A pair hard by
He found. The third some person sly
In deeper shade had hitched—more cool.
This was that mule whose rarer wine,
In pannier slung and blushing shy,
The Thessalonian did decline
Away with him in flight to take,
And friendly gave them when farewell he spake.

XXV

'Ah Rome, your tie ! may child clean part ?
Nay, tugs the mother at the heart ! '

    Strange voice that was which three there
       heard
Reclined upon the bank. They turned ;
And he, the speaker of the word,
Stood in the grass, with eyes that burned
How eloquent upon the group.
    ' Here urging on before our troop,'
He said, ' I caught your choral strains—
Spurred quicker, lighted, tied my mule
Behind yon clump ; and, for my pains,
Meet—three, I ween, who slight the rule
Of Rome, yet thence do here indeed,
Through strong compulsion of the need,
Derive fair rite : or may I err ? '
    Surprise they knew, yet made a stir
Of welcome, gazing on the man
In white robe of Dominican,
Of aspect strong, though cheek was spare,
Yellowed with tinge athlete may wear
Whom rigorous masters overtrain
When they with scourge of more and more
Would macerate him into power.
Inwrought herewith was yet the air
And open frontage frankly fair

271

Of one who 'd moved in active scene
And swayed men where they most convene.
His party came from Saba last,
Camping by Lot's wave overnight—
French pilgrims.   So he did recite
Being questioned.   Thereupon they passed
To matters of more pith.   Debate
They held, built on that hymning late ;
Till in reply to Derwent's strain
Thus warmed he, that Dominican :
        ' Crafty is Rome, you deem ?   Her art
Is simple, quarried from the heart.
Rough marbles, rudiments of worth
Ye win from ledges under earth ;
Ye trim them, fit them, make them shine
In structures of a fair design.
Well, fervours as obscure in birth—
Precious, though fleeting in their dates—
Rome culls, adapts, perpetuates
In ordered rites.   'Tis these supply
Means to the mass to beautify
The rude emotion ; lend meet voice
To organs which would fain rejoice
But lack the song ; and oft present
To sorrow bound, an instrument
Which liberates.   Each hope, each fear
Between the christening and the bier
Still Rome provides for, and with grace
And tact which hardly find a place
In uninspired designs.'
                        ' Let be,
Thou Paul ! shall Festus yield to thee ? '
Cried Rolfe ; ' and yet,' in altered tone,
' Even these fair things—ah, change goes
        on ! '

'Change ? yes, but not with us. In rout
Sword-hilts rap at the Vatican,
And, lo, an old, old man comes out :
" What would ye ? "   " Change ! "   " I never
    change." '
    ' Things changing not when all things change
Need perish then, one might retort,
Nor err.'
          ' Ay, things of human sort.'
      ' Rome superhuman ? '
                ' As ye will.
Brave schemes these boyish times instil ;
But Rome has lived a thousand years :
Shall not a thousand years know more
Than nonage may ? '   ' Then all the cheers
Which hail the good time deemed at door
Are but the brayings which attest
The foolish, many-headed beast ! '
' Hardly that inference I own.
The people once elected me
To be their spokesman.   In this gown
I sat in legislative hall
A champion of true liberty—
God's liberty for one and all—
Not Satan's licence.   Mine 's the state
Of a staunch Catholic Democrat.'
    Indulgent here was Derwent's smile,
Incredulous was Rolfe's.   But he :
' Hardly those terms ye reconcile.
And yet what is it that we see ?
Before the Church our human race
Stand equal.   None attain to place
Therein through claim of birth or fee.
No monk so mean but he may dare
Aspire to sit in Peter's chair.'

'Why, true,' said Derwent ; ' but what
    then ?
That sums not all.   And what think men ? '
And, briefly, more, about the rot
Of Rome in Luther's time, the canker spot.
    'Well,' said the monk, ' I 'll not gainsay
Some things you put : I own the shame :
Reform was needed, yes, and came—
Reform *within*.   But let that go—
That era 's gone : how fares it *now* ?—
Melancthon ! was forecast by thee,
Who fain had tempered Luther's mind,
This riot of reason quite set free :
Sects—sects bisected—sects disbanded
Into plain deists underhanded ?
Against all this stands Rome's array :
Rome is the Protestant to-day :
The Red Republic slinging flame
In Europe—she 's your Scarlet Dame.
Rome stands ; but who may tell the end ?
Relapse barbaric may impend,
Dismission into ages blind—
Moral dispersion of mankind.
Ah, God,' and dropped upon the knee :
' These flocks which range so far from Thee,
Ah, leave them not to be undone :
Let them not cower as 'twixt the sea
And storm—in panic crowd and drown ! '
He rose, resumed his previous cheer
With something of a bearing sweet.
    ' Brother,' said Derwent friendly here,
' I 'm glad to know ye, glad to meet,
Even though, in part, your Rome seeks ends
Not mine.   But see, there pass your friends :
Call they your name ? '

                   ' Yes, yes,' he said,
And rose to loose his mule ; ' you 're right ;
We go to win the further bed
Of Jordan, by the convent's site.
A parting word : Methinks ye hold
Reserved objections.   I 'll unfold
But one :—Rome being fixed in form,
Unyielding there, how may she keep
Adjustment with new times ?   But deep
Below rigidities of form
The invisible nerves and tissues change
Adaptively.   As men that range
From clime to clime, from zone to zone
(Say Russian hosts that menace Ind)
Through all vicissitudes still find
The body acclimate itself
While form and function hold their own.
Again they call :—Well, you are wise ;
Enough—you can analogise
And take my meaning : I have done.
No, one more point :—Science but deals
With Nature ; Nature is not God ;
Never she answers our appeals,
Or, if she do, but mocks the clod.
Call to the echo—it returns
The word you send ; how thrive the ferns
About the ruined house of prayer
In woods ; one shadow falleth yet
From Christian spire—Turk minaret :
Consider the indifference there.
'Tis so throughout.   Shall Science then,
Which solely dealeth with this thing
Named Nature, shall she ever bring
One solitary hope to men ?
'Tis Abba Father that we seek,

Not the Artificer. I speak,
But scarce may utter. Let it be.
Adieu ; remember—Oh, not me ;
But if with years should fail delight
As things unmask abroad and home ;
Then, should ye yearn in reason's spite,
Remember hospitable Rome.'

He turned, and would have gone ; but, no,
New matter struck him : ' Ere I go
Yet one word more ; and bear with me :
Whatever your belief may be—
If well ye wish to human kind,
Be not so mad, unblest, and blind
As, in such days as these, to try
To pull down Rome. If Rome could fall
'Twould not be Rome alone, but all
Religion. All with Rome have tie,
Even the railers which deny,
All but the downright Anarchist,
Christ-hater, Red, and Vitriolist.
Could libertine dreams true hope disable,
Rome's tomb would prove Abaddon's cradle.
Weigh well the Pope. Though he should be
Despoiled of Charlemagne's great fee—
Cast forth, and made a begging friar,
That would not quell him. No, the higher
Rome's *In excelsis* would extol
Her God—her *De profundis* roll
The deeper. Let destructives mind
The reserves upon reserves behind.
Offence I mean not. More 's to tell :
But frigates meet—hail—part. Farewell.'
And, going, he a verse did weave,
Or hummed in low recitative :

' Yearly for a thousand years
On Christmas Day the wreath appears,
    And the people joy together :
Prithee, Prince or Parliament,
An equal holiday invent
    Outlasting centuries of weather.

' Arrested by a trembling shell,
Wee tinkle of the small mass-bell,
    A giant drops upon the knee.
Thou art wise—effect as much ;
Let thy wisdom by a touch
    Reverence like this decree.'

XXVI

OF ROME

'PATCHER of the rotten cloth,
Pickler of the wing o' the moth,
Toaster of bread stale in date,
Tinker of the rusty plate,
Botcher of a crumbling tomb,
Pounder with the holy hammer,
Gaffer-gammer, gaffer-gammer—
Rome!
The broker take your trumpery pix,
Paten and chalice! Turn ye—lo,
Here 's bread, here 's wine. In Mexico
Earthquakes lay flat your crucifix:
All, all 's geology, I trow.
Away to your Pope Joan—go!'

As he the robed one decorous went,
From copse that doggerel was sent
And after-cry. Half screened from view
'Twas Margoth, who, reclined at lunch,
Had overheard, nor spared to munch,
And thence his contumely threw.
Rolfe, rising, had replied thereto,
And with some heat, but Derwent's hand
Caught at his skirt: 'Nay, of what use?
But wind, foul wind.'—Here fell a truce,
Which Margoth could but understand;

Wiping his mouth he hied away.
The student who apart though near
Had heard the Frank with tingling cheer,
Awaited now the after-play
Of comment ; and it followed : ' Own,'
Said Rolfe, ' he took no shallow tone,
That new St. Dominick.   Who 'll repay ?
Wilt thou ? ' to Derwent turning.—' No,
Not I ! But had our Scot been near
To meet your Papal nuncio !
Fight fire with fire.   But for me here,
You must have marked I did abstain.—
Odd, odd : this man who 'd make our age
To Hildebrand's an appanage—
So able too—lit by our light—
Curious, he should so requite !
And, yes, lurked somewhat in his strain——'
      ' And in his falling on the knee ? '
' Those supple hinges I let be.'
      ' Is the man false ? '
                              ' No, hardly that.
'Tis difficult to tell.   But see :
Doubt late was an aristocrat ;
But now the barbers' clerks do swell
In cast clothes of the infidel ;
The more then one can now *believe*,
The more one 's differenced, perceive,
From ribald commonplace.   Here Rome
Comes in.   This intellectual man—
Half monk, half tribune, partisan—
Who, as he hints—'tis troublesome
To analyse, and thankless too :
Much better be a dove, and coo
Softly.   Come then, I 'll e'en agree
His manner has a certain lure,

Disinterested, earnest, pure
And liberal. 'Tis such as he
Win over men.'
                    ' There 's Rome, her camp
Of tried instruction. She can stamp,
On the recruit that 's framed aright,
The bearing of a Bayard knight
Ecclesiastic. I applaud
Her swordsmen of the priestly sword
Wielded in spiritual fight.'
' Indeed ? take care ! Rome lacks not charm
For fervid souls. Arm ye, forearm !
For syrens has she too—her race
Of sainted virgin ones, with grace
Beyond the grace of Grecian calm,
For this is chill, but that how warm.'
' A frank concession.' ' To be sure !
Since Rome may never *me* allure
By her enticing arts ; since all
The bias of the days that be
Away leans from Authority,
And most when hierarchical ;
So that the future of the Pope
Is cast in no fair horoscope ;
In brief, since Rome must still decay,
Less care I to disown or hide
Aught that she has of merit rare :
Her legends—some are sweet as May ;
Ungarnered wealth no doubt is there
(Too long ignored by Luther's pride),
But which perchance in days divine
(Era, whereof I read the sign)
When much that sours the sects is gone,
Like Dorian myths the bards shall own—
Yes, prove the poet's second mine.'

' All that,' said Rolfe, ' is very fine ;
But Rome subsists, she lives to-day,
She re-affirms herself, her sway
Seductive draws rich minds away ;
Some pastures, too, yield many a rover :
Sheep, sheep and shepherd running over.'

   ' Such sheep and shepherds, let them go ;
They are not legion : and you know
What draws. Little imports it all
Overbalanced by that tidal fall
Of Rome in Southern Europe. Come.'

   ' If the tide fall or here or there,
Be sure 'tis rolling in elsewhere.'

   ' So oceanic then is Rome ? '

' Nay, but there 's ample sea-verge left :
A hemisphere invites.—When reft
From Afric, and the East its home,
The Church shot out through wild and
       wood—
Germany, Gaul and Britain, Spain—
Colonised, Latinised, and made good
Her loss, and more—resolved to reign.'

   ' Centuries, centuries long ago !
What 's that to us ? I am surprised.
Rome's guns are spiked ; and they 'll stay so.
The world is now too civilised
For Rome. Your noble Western soil—
What ! *that* be given up for spoil
To—to——'

        ' There is an Unforeseen.
Fate never gives a guarantee
That she 'll abstain from aught. And men
Get tired at last of being free—
Whether in states—in states or creeds.
For what 's the sequel ? Verily,

Laws scribbled by law-breakers, creeds
Scrawled by the freethinkers, and deeds
Shameful and shameless. Men get sick
Under that curse of Frederic
The cynical : For punishment
This rebel province I present
To the philosophers. But, how ?
Whole nations now philosophise,
And do their own undoing now.—
Who 's gained by all the sacrifice
Of Europe's revolutions ? who ?
The Protestant ? the Liberal ?
I do not think it—not at all :
Rome and the Atheist have gained :
These two shall fight it out—these two ;
Protestantism being retained
For base of operations sly
By Atheism.'
              Without reply
Derwent low whistled—twitched a spray
That overhung : ' What tree is this ? '
    ' The tree of knowledge, I dare say ;
But you don't eat.'—' That 's not amiss,'
The good man laughed ; but, changing, ' Oh,
That a New-Worlder should talk so ! '
    ' 'Tis the New World that mannered me,
Yes, gave me this vile liberty
To reverence naught, not even herself.'
    ' How say you ? you 're the queerest elf !
But here 's a thought I still pursue—
A thought I dreamed each thinker knew :
No more can men be what they 've been ;
All 's altered—earth 's another scene.'
    ' Man's heart is what it used to be.'
' I don't know that.'

' But Rome does, though :
And hence her stout persistency.
What mean her re-adopted modes
Even in the enemy's abodes ?
Their place old emblems reassume.
She bides—content to let but blow
Among the sects that peak and pine,
Incursions of her taking bloom.'
   ' The censer's musk ?—'Tis not the vine,
Vine evangelic, branching out
In fruitful latitude benign,
With all her bounty round about—
Each cluster, shaded or in sun,
Still varying from each other one,
But all true members, all with wine
Derived from Christ their stem and stock ;
'Tis scarce *that* vine which doth unlock
The fragrance that you hint of.   No,
The Latin plant don't flourish so ;
Of sad distemper 'tis the seat ;
Pry close, and startled you shall meet
Parasite-bugs—black swarming ones.'
' The monks ? '—' You jest : thinned out, those
       drones.'
   Considerate uncommitted eyes
Charged with things manifold and wise,
Rolfe turned upon good Derwent here ;
Then changed : ' Fall back we must.   Yon mule
With pannier : Come, in stream we 'll cool
The wine ere quaffing.—Muleteer ! '

XXVII

VINE AND CLAREL

WHILE now, to serve the pilgrim train,
The Arabs willow branches hew
(For palms they serve in dearth of true),
Or, kneeling by the margin, stoop
To brim memorial bottles up ;
And the Greek's wine entices two :
Apart see Clarel here incline,
Perplexed by that Dominican,
Nor less by Rolfe—capricious man :
' I cannot penetrate him.—Vine ? '

    As were Venetian slats between,
He espied him through a leafy screen,
Luxurious there in umbrage thrown,
Light sprays above his temples blown—
The river through the green retreat
Hurrying, revelling by his feet.

    Vine looked an overture, but said
Nothing, till Clarel leaned—half laid—
Beside him : then ' We dream, or be
In sylvan John's baptistery :
May Pisa's equal beauty keep ?—
But how bad habits persevere !
I have been moralising here
Like any imbecile : as thus :
Look how these willows overweep
The waves, and plain : " Fleet so from us ?
And wherefore ? whitherward away ?
Your best is here where wildings sway

And the light shadow 's blown about ;
Ah, tarry, for at hand 's a sea
Whence ye shall never issue out
Once in." They sing back : " So let be !
We madcaps hymn it as we flow—
Short life and merry ! be it so ! " '
   Surprised at such a fluent turn,
The student did but listen—learn.

   Putting aside the twigs which screened,
Again Vine spake, and lightly leaned :
' Look ; in yon vault so leafy dark,
At deep end lit by gemmy spark
Of mellowed sunbeam in a snare ;
Over the stream—ay, just through there—
The sheik on that celestial mare
Shot, fading.—Clan of outcast Hagar,
Well do ye come by spear and dagger !
Yet in your bearing ye outvie
Our western Red Men, chiefs that stalk
In mud paint—whirl the tomahawk.—
But in these Nimrods noted you
The natural language of the eye,
Burning or liquid, flame or dew,
As still the changeable quick mood
Made transit in the wayward blood ?
Methought therein one might espy,
For all the wildness, thoughts refined
By the old Asia's dreamful mind ;
But hark—a bird ? '
               Pure as the rain
Which diamondeth with lucid grain
The white swan in the April hours
Floating between two sunny showers
Upon the lake, while buds unroll ;

So pure, so virginal in shrine
Of true unworldliness looked Vine.
Ah, clear sweet ether of the soul
(Mused Clarel), holding him in view.
Prior advances unreturned
Not here he recked of, while he yearned—
Oh, now but for communion true
And close ; let go each alien theme ;
Give me thyself !
          But Vine, at will
Dwelling upon his wayward dream,
Nor as suspecting Clarel's thrill
Of personal longing, rambled still :
' Methinks they show a lingering trace
Of some quite unrecorded race
Such as the Book of Job implies.
What ages of refinings wise
Must have forerun what there is writ—
More ages than have followed it.
At Lydda late, as chance would have,
Some tribesmen from the south I saw,
Their tents pitched in the Gothic nave,
The ruined one. Disowning law,
Not lawless lived they ; no, indeed ;
Their chief—why, one of Sydney's clan,
A slayer, but chivalric man ;
And chivalry, with all that breed
Was Arabic or Saracen
In source, they tell. But, as men stray
Further from Ararat away
Pity it were did they recede
In carriage, manners, and the rest ;
But no, for ours the palm indeed
In bland amenities far West !
Come now, for pastime let 's complain ;

Grudged thanks, Columbus, for thy main !
Put back, as 'twere—assigned by fate
To fight crude Nature o'er again,
By slow degrees we re-create.
But then, alas, in Arab camps
No lack, they say, no lack of scamps.'
    Divided mind knew Clarel here ;
The heart's desire did interfere.
Thought he, How pleasant in another
Such sallies, or in thee, if said
After confidings that should wed
Our souls in one :—Ah, call me *brother* !—
So feminine his passionate mood
Which, long as hungering unfed,
All else rejected or withstood.
    Some inklings he let fall. But no :
Here over Vine there slid a change—
A shadow, such as thin may show
Gliding along the mountain-range
And deepening in the gorge below.
    Does Vine's rebukeful dusking say—
Why, on this vernal bank to-day,
Why bring oblations of thy pain
To one who hath his share ? here fain
Would lap him in a chance reprieve ?
Lives none can help ye ; that believe.
Art thou the first soul tried by doubt ?
Shalt prove the last ? Go, live it out.
But for thy fonder dream of love
In man toward man—the soul's caress—
The negatives of flesh should prove
Analogies of non-cordialness
In spirit.—E'en such conceits could cling
To Clarel's dream of vain surmise
And imputation full of sting.

But, glancing up, unwarned he saw
What serious softness in those eyes
Bent on him. Shyly they withdraw.
Enslaver, wouldst thou but fool me
With bitter-sweet, sly sorcery,
Pride's pastime ? or would'st thou indeed,
Since things unspoken may impede,
Let flow thy nature but for bar ?
Nay, dizzard, sick these feelings are ;
How findest place within thy heart
For such solicitudes apart
From Ruth ?—Self-taxings.
                                    But a sign
Came here indicative from Vine,
Who with a reverent hushed air
His view directed toward the glade
Beyond, wherein a niche was made
Of leafage, and a kneeler there,
The meek one, on whom, as he prayed,
A golden shaft of mellow light,
Oblique through vernal cleft above,
And making his pale forehead bright,
Scintillant fell. By such a beam
From heaven descended erst the dove
On Christ emerging from the stream.
It faded ; 'twas a transient ray ;
And, quite unconscious of its sheen,
The suppliant rose and moved away,
Not dreaming that he had been seen.

When next they saw that innocent,
From prayer such cordial had he won
That all his aspect of content
As with the oil of gladness shone.
Less aged looked he. And his cheer

Took language in an action here :
The train now mustering in line,
Each pilgrim with a river-palm
In hand (except indeed the Jew),
The saint the headstall need entwine
With wreathage of the same.   When new
They issued from the wood, no charm
The ass found in such idle gear
Superfluous : with her long ear
She flapped it off, and the next thrust
Of hoof imprinted it in dust.
Meek hands (mused Vine), vainly ye twist
Fair garland for the realist.

  The Hebrew, noting whither bent
Vine's glance, a word in passing lent :
' Ho, tell us how it comes to be
That thou who rank'st not with beginners
Regard have for yon chief of sinners.'

  ' Yon chief of sinners ? '

         ' So names he
Himself.   For one I 'll not express
How I do loathe such lowliness.'

THE FOG

SOUTHWARD they file. 'Tis Pluto's park
Beslimed as after baleful flood :
A nitrous, filmed and pallid mud,
With shrubs to match. Salt specks they mark
Or mildewed stunted twigs unclean
Brushed by the stirrup, Stygian green,
With shrivelled nut or apple small.
⠀⠀⠀⠀The Jew plucked one. Like a fuzz-ball
It brake, discharging fetid dust.
⠀⠀⠀⠀' Pippins of Sodom ? they 've declined ! '
Cried Derwent : ' where 's the ruddy rind ? '
⠀⠀⠀⠀Said Rolfe : ' If Circe tempt one thus,
A fig for vice—I 'm virtuous.
Who but poor Margoth now would lust
After such fruitage. See, but see
What makes our Nehemiah to be
So strange. That looks returns to him
Which late he wore by Achor's rim.'

⠀⠀⠀⠀Over pale hollows foully smeared
The saint hung with an aspect weird :
' Yea, here it was the kings were tripped,
These, these the slime-pits where they slipped—
Gomorrah's lord and Sodom's, lo ! '

⠀⠀⠀⠀' *What 's* that ? ' asked Derwent.
⠀⠀⠀⠀⠀⠀⠀⠀⠀⠀⠀⠀⠀⠀⠀⠀⠀⠀' You should know,'
Said Rolfe : ' your Scripture lore revive :
290

The four kings strove against the five
In Siddim here.'
          ' Ah—Genesis.
But turn ; upon this other hand
See here another not remiss.'
      'Twas Margoth raking there the land.
Some minerals of noisome kind
He found and straight to pouch consigned.
    ' The chiffonier ! ' cried Rolfe ; ' e'en grim
Milcom and Chemosh scowl at him—
Here nosing underneath their lee
Of pagod heights.'
         In deeper dale
What canker may their palms assail ?
Spotted they show, all limp they be.
Is it thy bitter mist, Bad Sea,
That, sudden driving, northward comes
Involving them, that each man roams
Half seen or lost ?
         But in the dark
Thick scud, the chanting saint they hark :

    ' Though through the valley of the shade
      I pass, no evil do I fear ;
   His candle shineth on my head :
      Lo, He is with me, even here.'

    The rack drove by : and Derwent said—
' How apt he is ! ' then pause he made :
' This palm has grown a sorry sight ;
A palm 'tis not, if named aright :
I 'll drop it.—Look, the lake ahead ! '

XXIX

THE legend round a Grecian urn,
The sylvan legend, though decay
Have wormed the garland all away,
And fire have left its Vandal burn ;
Yet beauty inextinct may charm
In outline of the vessel's form.
Much so with Sodom, shore and sea.
Fair Como would like Sodom be
Should horror overrun the scene
And calcine all that makes it green,
Yet haply sparing to impeach
The contour in its larger reach.
In graceful lines the hills advance,
The valley's sweep repays the glance,
And wavy curves of winding beach ;
But all is charred or crunched or riven,
Scarce seems of earth whereon we dwell ;
Though framed within the lines of heaven
The picture intimates a hell.
        That marge they win.   Bides Mortmain
            there ?
No trace of man, not anywhere.
        It was the salt wave's northern brink.
No gravel bright nor shell was seen,
Nor kelpy growth nor coralline,
But dead boughs stranded, which the rout
Of Jordan, in old freshets born
In Libanus, had madly torn

Green from her arbour and thrust out
Into the liquid waste. No sound
Nor motion but of sea. The land
Was null : nor bramble, weed, nor trees,
Nor anything that grows on ground,
Flexile to indicate the breeze ;
Though hitherward by south winds fanned
From Usdum's brink and Bozrah's site
Of bale, flew gritty atoms light.
Toward Karek's castle lost in blur,
And thence beyond toward Aroer
By Arnon where the robbers keep,
Jackal and vulture, eastward sweep
The waters, while their western rim
Stretches by Judah's headlands grim,
Which make in turns a sea-wall steep.
There, by the cliffs or distance hid,
The Fount or Cascade of the Kid
An Eden mades of one high glen,
One vernal and contrasted scene
In jaws of gloomy crags uncouth—
Rosemary in the black boar's mouth.
Alike withheld from present view
(And, until late, but hawk and kite
Visited the forgotten site).
The Maccabees' Masada true ;
Stronghold which Flavian arms did rend,
The Peak of Eleazer's end,
Where patriot warriors made with brides
A martyrdom of suicides.
There too did Mariamne's hate
The death of John accelerate.
A crag of fairest, foulest weather—
Famous and infamous together.

  Hereof they spake, but never Vine,

Who little knew or seemed to know
Derived from books, but did incline
In docile way to each one's flow
Of knowledge bearing anyhow
In points less noted.
                              Southernmost
The sea indefinite was lost
Under a catafalque of cloud.
        Unwelcome impress to disown
Or light evade, the priest, aloud
Taking an interested tone
And brisk, ' Why, yonder lies Mount Hor,
E'en thereaway—that southward shore.'
        ' Ay,' added Rolfe, ' and Aaron's cell
Thereon.   A mountain sentinel,
He holds in solitude austere
The outpost of prohibited Seir
In cut-off Edom.'
                        ' God can sever ! '
Brake in the saint, who nigh them stood ;
' The satyr to the dragon's brood
Crieth !   God's word abideth ever :
None there pass through—no, never, never ! '
        ' My friend Max Levi, he passed through.'
They turned.   It was the hardy Jew.
Absorbed in vision here, the saint
Heard not.   The priest in flushed constraint
Showed mixed emotion ; part he winced
And part a humour pleased evinced—
Relish that would from qualms be free—
Aversion involved with sympathy.
But changing, and in formal way—
' Admitted ; nay, 'tis tritely true ;
Men pass thro' Edom, through and through.
But surely, few so dull to-day

As not to make allowance meet
For Orientalism's play
In Scripture, where the chapters treat
Of mystic themes.'
                With eye askance,
The apostate fixed no genial glance :
' Ay, Keith 's grown obsolete. And, pray,
How long will these last glosses stay ?
The agitating influence
Of knowledge never will dispense
With teasing faith, do what ye may.
Adjust and readjust, ye deal
With compass in a ship of steel.'
    ' Such perturbations do but give
Proof that faith 's vital : sensitive
Is faith, my friend.'
                ' Go to, go to :
Your black bat ! how she hangs askew,
Torpid, from wall by claws of wings :
Let drop the left—sticks fast the right ;
Then this unhook—the other swings ;
Leave—she regains her double plight.'
    ' Ah, look,' cried Derwent ; ' ah, behold ! '
From the blue battlements of air,
Over saline vapours hovering there,
A flag was flung out—curved in fold—
Fiery, rosy, violet, green—
And, lovelier growing, brighter, fairer,
Transfigured all that evil scene ;
And Iris was the standard-bearer.
      None spake. As in a world made new,
With upturned faces they review
That oriflamme, the which no man
Would look for in such clime of ban.
'Twas northern ; and its home-like look

Touched Nehemiah.   He, late with book
Gliding from Margoth's dubious sway,
Was standing by the ass apart ;
And when he caught that scarf of May
How many a year ran back his heart :
Scythes hang in orchard, haycocks loom
After eve-showers, the mossed roofs gloom
Greenly beneath the homestead trees ;
He tingles with these memories.

    For Vine, over him suffusive stole
An efflorescence ; all the soul
Flowering in flush upon the brow.
But 'twas ambiguously replaced
In words addressed to Clarel now—
' Yonder the arch dips in the waste ;
Thither ! and win the pouch of gold.'

    Derwent reproached him : ' Ah, withhold !
See, even death's pool reflects the dyes—
The rose upon the coffin lies ! '

    ' Brave words,' said Margoth, plodding near ;
' Brave words ; but yonder bow 's forsworn.
The covenant made on Noah's morn,
Was that well kept ? why, hardly here,
Where whelmed by fire and flood, they say,
The townsfolk sank in after day,
Yon sign in heaven should reappear.'

    They heard, but in such torpid gloom
Scarcely they recked, for now the bloom
Vanished from sight, and half the sea
Died down to glazed monotony.

    Craved solace here would Clarel prove,
Recalling Ruth, her glance of love.
But nay ; those eyes so frequent known
To meet, and mellow on his own—
Now, in his vision of them, swerved ;

While in perverse recurrence ran
Dreams of the bier Armenian.
Against their sway his soul he nerved :
' Go, goblins ; go, each funeral thought—
Bewitchment from this Dead Sea caught ! '

Westward they move, and turn the shore
Southward, till, where wild rocks are set,
Dismounting, they would fain restore
Ease to the limb. But haunts them yet
A dumb dejection lately met.

XXX

'THE City Red in cloud-land lies
Yonder,' said Derwent, quick to inter
The ill, or light regard transfer :
' But Petra must we leave unseen—
Tell us '—to Rolfe—' there hast thou been.'
   ' With dragons guarded round about
'Twas a new Jason found her out—
Burckhardt, you know.' ' But tell.' ' The flume
Or mountain corridor profound
Whereby ye win the inner ground
Petræan ; this, from purple gloom
Of cliffs—whose tops the suns illume
Where oleanders wave the flag—
Winds out upon the rosy stain,
Warm colour of the natural vein,
Of porch and pediment in crag.
One starts. In Esau's waste are blent
Ionian form, Venetian tint.
Statues salute ye from that fane,
The warders of the Horite lane.
They welcome, seem to point ye on
Where sequels which transcend them dwell ;
But tarry, for just here is won
Happy suspension of the spell.'
   ' But expectation 's raised.'
                     ' No more !
'Tis then when bluely blurred in shore,

It looms through azure haze at sea—
Then most 'tis Colchis charmeth ye.
So ever, and with all ! But, come,
Imagine us now quite at home
Taking the prospect from Mount Hor.
Good. Eastward turn thee—skipping o'er
The intervening craggy blight :
Mark'st thou the face of yon slabbed height
Shouldered about by heights ? what Door
Is that, sculptured in elfin freak ?
The portal of the Prince o' the Air ?
Thence will the god emerge, and speak ?
El Deir it is ; and Petra 's there,
Down in her cleft. Mid such a scene
Of Nature's terror, how serene
That ordered form. Nor less 'tis cut
Out of that terror—does abut
Thereon : there 's Art.'

    ' Dare say—no doubt ;
But, prithee, turn we now about
And closer get thereto in mind ;
That portal lures me.'

    ' Nay, forbear ;
A bootless journey. We should wind
Along ravine by mountain-stair—
Down which in season torrents sweep—
Up, slant by sepulchres in steep,
Grotto and porch, and so get near
Puck's platform, and thereby El Deir.
We 'd knock. An echo. Knock again—
Ay, knock forever : none requite :
The live spring filters through cell, fane,
And tomb : a dream the Edomite ! '

 ' And dreamers all who dream of him—
Though Sinbad 's pleasant in the skim.

Pæstum and Petra : good to use
For sedative when one would muse.
But look, our Emir.—Ay, Djalea,
We guess why thou com'st mutely here
And hintful stand'st before us so.'
  ' Ay, ay,' said Rolfe ; ' stirrups, and go ! '
' But first,' the priest said, ' let me creep
And rouse our poor friend slumbering low
Under yon rock—queer place to sleep.'

' *Queer ?* ' muttered Rolfe as Derwent went ;
' *Queer* is the furthest he will go
In phrase of a disparagement.
But—ominous, with haggard rent—
To me yon crag's browbeating brow
Looks horrible—and I *say* so.'

XXXI

WHILE yet Rolfe's foot in stirrup stood,
Ere the light vault that wins the seat,
Derwent was heard : ' What 's this we meet ?
A Cross ? and—if one could but spell—
Inscription Sinaitic ?   Well,
Mortmain is nigh—*his* crazy freak ;
Whose else ?   A closer view I 'll seek ;
I 'll climb.'
          In moving there aside
The rock's turned brow he had espied ;
In rear this rock hung o'er the waste
And Nehemiah in sleep embraced
Below.   The forepart gloomed Lot's wave
So nigh, the tide the base did lave.
Above, the sea-face smooth was worn
Through long attrition of that grit
Which on the waste of winds is borne.
And on the tablet high of it—
Traced in dull chalk, such as is found
Accessible in upper ground—
Big there between two scrawls, below
And over—a cross ; three stars in row
Upright, two more for thwarting limb
Which drooped oblique.
             At Derwent's cry
The rest drew near ; and every eye
Marked the device.—Thy passion's whim,

301

Wild Swede, mused Vine in silent heart.
' Looks like the *Southern Cross* to me,'
Said Clarel ; ' so 'tis down in chart.'
' And so,' said Rolfe, ' 'tis set in sky—
Though error slight of place prevail
In midmost star here chalked.   At sea,
Bound for Peru, when south ye sail,
Startling that novel cluster strange
Peers up from low ; then as ye range
Cape-ward still further, brightly higher
And higher the stranger doth aspire,
'Till off the Horn, when at full height
Ye slack your gaze as chilly grows the night.
But Derwent—see ! '

                The priest having gained
Convenient lodge the text below,
They called : ' What 's that in curve contained
Above the stars ?   Read : we would know.'
' Runs thus : *By one who wails the loss,*
This altar to the Slanting Cross.'
' Ha ! under that ? '   ' Some crow's-foot scrawl.'
' Decipher, quick ! we 're waiting all.'
' Patience : for ere one try rehearse,
'Twere well to make it out.   'Tis verse.'
' Verse, say you ?   Read.'   ' 'Tis mystical :

    ' " Emblazoned bleak in austral skies—
    A heaven remote, whose starry swarm
    Like Science lights but cannot warm—
    Translated Cross, hast thou withdrawn,
    Dim paling too at every dawn,
    With symbols vain once counted wise,
    And gods declined to heraldries ?
    Estranged, estranged : can friend prove so ?
    Aloft, aloof, a frigid sign :

How far removed, thou Tree divine,
Whose tender fruit did reach so low—
Love apples of New Paradise !
About the wide Australian sea
The planted nations yet to be—
When, ages hence, they lift their eyes,
Tell, what shall they retain of thee ?
But class thee with Orion's sword ?
In constellations unadored,
Christ and the Giant equal prize ?
The atheist cycles—*must* they be ?
Fomentors as forefathers we ? " '

   ' Mad, mad enough,' the priest here cried,
Down slipping by the shelving brinks ;
' But 'tis not Mortmain,' and he sighed.
   ' Not Mortmain ? ' Rolfe exclaimed. ' Methinks,'
The priest, ' 'tis hardly in his vein.'
' How ? fraught with feeling is the strain ?
His heart 's not ballasted with stone—
He 's crank.' ' Well, well, e'en let us own
That Mortmain, Mortmain is the man.
We 've then a pledge here at a glance
Our comrade 's met with no mischance.
Soon he 'll rejoin us.' ' There, amen ! '
' But now to wake Nehemiah in den
Behind here.—But kind Clarel goes.
Strange how he naps nor trouble knows
Under the crag's impending block,
Nor fears its fall, nor recks of shock.'

   Anon they mount ; and much advance
Upon that chalked significance.
The student harks, and weighs each word,
Intent, he being newly stirred.

But tarries Margoth ? Yes, behind
He lingers. He placards his mind :
Scaling the crag he rudely scores
With the same chalk (how here abused !)
Left by the other, after used,
A sledge or hammer huge as Thor's ;
A legend lending—this, to wit :
' *I, Science, I whose gain 's thy loss,*
I slanted thee, thou Slanting Cross.'
But sun and rain, and wind, with grit
Driving, these haste to cancel it.

XXXII

THE ENCAMPMENT

SOUTHWARD they find a strip at need
Between the mount and marge, and make.
In expectation of the Swede,
Encampment there, nor shun the Lake.
'Twas afternoon. With Arab zest
The Bethlehemites their spears present,
Whereon they lift and spread the tent
And care for all.
                        As Rolfe from rest
Came out, toward early eventide,
His comrades sat the shore beside,
In shadow deep, which from the west
The main Judæan mountains flung.
That ridge they faced, and anxious hung
Awaiting Mortmain, some having grown
The more concerned, because from stone
Inscribed, they had indulged a hope :
But now in ill surmise they grope.
Anew they question grave Djalea.
But what knows *he* ?
                        Their hearts to cheer,
' Trust,' Derwent said, ' hope's silver bell ;
Nor dream he 'd do his life a wrong—
No, never ! '
                        ' Demons here which dwell,'
Cried Rolfe, ' riff-raff of Satan's throng,
May fetch him steel, rope, poison—well,

He 'd spurn them, hoot their scurvy hell :
There 's nobler.—But what *other* knell
Of hap——' He turned him toward the sea.
　　Like leagues of ice which slumberous roll
About the pivot of the pole—
Vitreous—glass it seemed to be.
Beyond, removed in air sublime,
As 'twere some more than human clime,
In flanking towers of Ætna hue
The Ammonitish mounts they view
Enkindled by the sunset cast
Over Judah's ridgy headlands massed
Which blacken baseward.　Ranging higher
Where vague glens pierced the steeps of fire,
Imagination time repealed—
Restored there, and in fear revealed
Lot and his daughters twain in flight,
Three shadows flung on reflex light
Of Sodom in her funeral pyre.
　　Some fed upon the natural scene,
Deriving many a wandering hint
Such as will oft-times intervene
When on the slab ye view the print
Of perished species.—Judge Rolfe's start
And quick revulsion, when, apart,
Derwent he saw at ease reclined,
With page before him, page refined
And appetising, which threw ope
New parks, fresh walks for Signor Hope
To saunter in.
　　　　　　　' And read you here ?
Scarce suits the ground with bookish cheer.
Escaped from forms, enlarged at last,
Pupils we be of wave and waste—
Not books ; nay, nay ! '

                    ' Book-comment, though,'—
Smiled Derwent—' were it ill to know ? '
      ' But how if Nature vetoes all
Her commentators ?   Disenthral
Thy heart.   Look round.   Are not here
            met
Books and that truth no type shall set ? '—
Then, to himself in refluent flow :
' Earnest again !—well, let it go.'
          Derwent quick glanced from face to face,
Lighting upon the student's hue
Of pale perplexity, with trace
Almost of twinge at Rolfe : ' Believe,
Though here I random page review,
Not books I let exclusive cleave
And sway.   Much too there is, I grant,
Which well might Solomon's wisdom daunt—
Much that we mark.   Nevertheless,
Were it a paradox to confess
A book 's a man ?   If this be so,
Books be but part of Nature.   Oh,
'Tis studying Nature, reading books :
And 'tis through Nature each heart looks
Up to a God, or whatsoe'er
One images beyond our sphere.
Moreover, Siddim 's not the world :
There 's Naples.   Why, yourself well know
What breadths of beauty lie unfurled
All round the bays where sailors go.
So, prithee, do not be severe,
But let me read.'
                    Rolfe looked esteem :
' You suave St. Francis !   Him, I mean,
Of Sales, not that soul whose dream
Founded the barefoot Order lean.

Though wise as serpents, Sales proves
The throbbings sweet of social doves.
I like you.'
                    Derwent laughed ; then, ' Ah
From each Saint Francis am I far ! '
And grave he grew.
                    It was a scene
Which Clarel in his memory scored :
How reconcile Rolfe's wizard chord
And forks of esoteric fire,
With commonplace of laxer mien ?
May truth be such a spendthrift lord ?
Then Derwent : he reviewed in heart
His tone with Margoth ; his attire
Of tolerance ; the easy part
He played.   Could Derwent, having gained
A certain slant in liberal thought,
Think there to bide, like one detained
Half-way adown the slippery glacier caught ?
Was honesty his, with lore and art
Not to be fooled ?—But if in vain
One tries to comprehend a man,
How think to sound God's deeper heart !

XXXIII

LOT'S SEA

Roving along the winding verge
Trying these problems as a lock,
Clarel upon the further marge
Caught sight of Vine. Upon a rock
Low couchant there, and dumb as that,
Bent on the wave Vine moveless sat.
The student after pause drew near :
Then, as in presence which though mute
Did not repel, without salute
He joined him.
    Unto these, by chance,
In ruminating slow advance
Came Rolfe, and lingered.
      At Vine's feet
A branchless tree lay lodged ashore,
One end immersed. Of form complete—
Half fossilised—could this have been,
In ages back, a palm-shaft green ?
Yes, long detained in depths which store
A bitter virtue, there it lay,
Washed up to sight—free from decay
But dead.
    And now in slouched return
From random prowlings, brief sojourn
As chance might prompt, the Jew they espy
Coasting inquisitive the shore
And frequent stooping. Ranging nigh,
In hirsute hand a flint he bore—

A flint, or stone, of smooth dull gloom :
' A jewel ? not asphaltum—no :
Observe it, pray.   Methinks in show
'Tis like the flagging round that Tomb
Ye celebrate.'
                         Rolfe, glancing, said,
' I err, or 'twas from Siddim's bed
Or quarry here, those floor-stones came :
'Tis Stone-of-Moses called, they vouch ;
The Arabs know it by that name.
          ' Moses ? who 's Moses ? '   Into pouch
The lump he slipped ; while wistful here
Clarel in silence challenged Vine ;
But not responsive was Vine's cheer,
Discharged of every meaning sign.
          With motive, Rolfe the talk renewed :
' Yes, here it was the cities stood
That sank in reprobation.   See,
The scene and record well agree.'
          ' Tut, tut—tut, tut.   Of aqueous force,
Vent igneous, a shake or so,
One here perceives the sign—of course ;
All 's mere geology, you know.'
          ' Nay, how should one know that ? '
                              ' By sight,
Touch, taste—all senses in assent
Of common sense their parliament.
Judge now ; this lake, with outlet none
And into which five streams discharge
From south ; which east and west is
          shown
Walled in by Alps along the marge ;
North, in this lake, the waters end
Of Jordan—end here, or dilate
Rather, and so evaporate

From surface.   But do you attend ? '
  ' Most teachably.'
                      ' Well, now : assume
This lake was formed, even as they tell,
Then first when the Five Cities fell ;
Where, I demand, ere yet that doom,
Where emptied Jordan ? '
                           ' Who can say ?
Not I.'
          ' No, none.   A point I make,
Coeval are the stream and lake !
I say no more.'
                    As came that close
A hideous hee-haw horrible rose,
Rebounded in unearthly sort
From shore to shore, as if retort
From all the damned in Sodom's Sea
Out brayed at him.   ' Just God, what 's that ? '
' The ass,' breathed Vine, with tropic eye
Freakishly impish, nor less shy ;
Then, distant as before, he sat.
     Anew Rolfe turned toward Margoth then ;
' May not these levels high and low
Have undergone derangement when
The cities met their overthrow ?
Or say there was a lake at first—
A supposition not reversed
By Writ—a lake enlarged through doom
Which overtook the cities ?   Come ! '—
     The Jew, recovering from decline
Arising from late asinine
Applause, replied hereto in way
Eliciting from Rolfe—' Delay :
What knowest thou ? or what know I ?
Suspect you may ere yet you die

Or afterward perchance may learn,
That Moses' God is no mere Pam
With painted clubs, but true I AM.'
     ' Hog-Latin,' was the quick return ;
' Plague on that ass ! ' for here again
Brake in the pestilent refrain.
     Meanwhile, as if in a dissent
Not bordering their element,
Vine kept his place, aloof in air.
They could but part and leave him there :
The Hebrew railing as they went—
' Of all the dolorous dull men !
He 's like a poor nun's pining hen.
And *me* too : should I let it pass ?
Ass ? did he say it was the ass ? '
Hereat, timed like the clerk's *Amen*
Yet once more did the hee-haw free
Come in with new alacrity.

     Vine tarried ; and with fitful hand
Took bits of dead drift from the sand
And flung them to the wave, as one
Whose race of thought long since was run—
For whom the spots enlarge that blot the
          golden sun.

XXXIV

WHILE now at poise the wings of shade
Outstretched overhang each ridge and glade,
Mortmain descends from Judah's height
Through sally-port of minor glens :
Against the background of black dens
Blacker the figure glooms enhanced.
    Relieved from anxious fears, the group
In friendliness would have advanced
To greet, but shrank or fell adroop.
    Like Hecla ice inveined with marl
And frozen cinders showed his face
Rigid and darkened. Shunning parle
He seated him aloof in place,
Hands clasped about the knees drawn up
As round the cask the binding hoop—
Condensed in self, or like a seer
Unconscious of each object near,
While yet, informed, the nerve may reach
Like wire under wave to furthest beach.
    By what brook Cherith had he been,
Watching it shrivel from the scene—
Or voice aerial had heard,
That now he murmured the wild word :
' But, hectored by the impious years,
What god invoke, for leave to unveil
That gulf whither tend these modern fears,
And deeps over which men crowd the sail ?

Up, as possessed, he rose anon,
And crying to the beach went down :
' Repent ! repent in every land
Or hell's hot kingdom is at hand !
Yea, yea,
In pause of the artillery's boom,
While now the armed world holds its own,
The comet peers, the star dips down ;
Flicker the lamps in Syria's tomb,
While Anti-Christ and Atheist set
On Anarch the red coronet ! '

   ' Mad John,' sighed Rolfe, ' dost there betray
The dire *Vox Clamans* of our day ? '
    ' Why heed him ? ' Derwent breathed : ' alas !
Let him alone, and it will pass.—
What would he now ? ' Before the bay
Low bowed he there, with hand addressed
To scoop. ' Unhappy, hadst thou best ? '
Djalea it was ; then calling low
Unto a Bethlehemite whose brow
Was wrinkled like the bat's shrunk hide—
' Your salt-song, Beltha : warn and chide.'

   ' Would ye know what bitter drink
     They gave to Christ upon the Tree ?
Sip the wave that laps the brink
     Of Siddim : taste, and God keep ye !
It drains the hills where alum 's hid—
Drains the rock-salt's ancient bed ;
    Hither unto basin fall
     The torrents from the steeps of gall—
Here is Hades' watershed.
     Sinner, would ye that your soul
     Bitter were and like the pool ?

Sip the Sodom waters dead ;
  But never from thy heart shall haste
  The Marah—yea, the after-taste.'

He closed.—Arrested as he stooped,
Did Mortmain his pale hand recall ?
No ; undeterred the wave he scooped,
And tried it—madly tried the gall.

XXXV

In Piranezi's rarer prints,
Interiors measurelessly strange,
Where the distrustful thought may range
Misgiving still—what mean the hints ?
Stairs upon stairs which dim ascend
In series from plunged bastilles drear—
Pit under pit ; long tier on tier
Of shadowed galleries which impend
Over cloisters, cloisters without end ;
The height, the depth—the far, the near ;
Ring-bolts to pillars in vaulted lanes,
And dragging Rhadamanthine chains ;
These less of wizard influence lend
Than some allusive chambers closed.
    Those wards of hush are not disposed
In gibe of goblin fantasy—
Grimace—unclean diablerie :
Thy wings, Imagination, span
Ideal truth in fable's seat :
The thing implied is one with man,
His penetralia of retreat—
The heart, with labyrinths replete :
In freaks of intimation see
Paul's ' mystery of iniquity ' :
Involved indeed, a blur of dream ;
As, awed by scruple and restricted
In first design, or interdicted
By fate and warnings as might seem ;

The inventor miraged all the maze,
Obscured it with prudential haze ;
Nor less, if subject unto question,
The egg left, egg of the suggestion.
Dwell on those etchings in the night,
Those touches bitten in the steel
By aqua-fortis, till ye feel
The Pauline text in gray of light ;
Turn hither then and read aright.

For ye who green or gray retain
Childhood's illusion, or but feign ;
As bride and suite let pass a bier—
So pass the coming canto here.

XXXVI

SODOM

FULL night. The moon has yet to rise ;
The air oppresses, and the skies
Reveal beyond the lake afar
One solitary tawny star—
Complexioned so by vapours dim,
Whereof some hang above the brim
And nearer waters of the lake,
Whose bubbling air-beads mount and break
As charged with breath of things alive.

In talk about the Cities Five
Engulfed, on beach they linger late.
And he, the quaffer of the brine,
Puckered with that heart-wizening wine
Of bitterness, among them sate
Upon a camel's skull, late dragged
From forth the wave, the eye-pits slagged
With crusted salt.—' What star is yon ? '
And pointed to that single one
Befogged above the sea afar.
' It might be Mars, so red it shines,'
One answered ; ' duskily it pines
In this strange mist.'—' It is the star
Called Wormwood. Some hearts die in thrall
Of waters which yon star makes gall ' ;
And, lapsing, turned, and made review
Of what that wickedness might be

Which down on these ill precincts drew
The flood, the fire ; put forth new plea,
Which not with Writ might disagree ;
Urged that those malefactors stood
Guilty of sins scarce scored as crimes
In any statute known, or code—
Nor now, nor in the former times :
Things hard to prove : decorum's wile,
Malice discreet, judicious guile ;
Good done with ill intent—reversed :
Best deeds designed to serve the worst ;
And hate which under life's fair hue
Prowls like the shark in sunned Pacific blue.
    He paused, and under stress did bow,
Lank hands enlocked across the brow.
    ' Nay, nay, thou sea,
'Twas not all carnal harlotry,
But sins refined, crimes of the spirit,
Helped earn that doom ye here inherit :
Doom well imposed, though sharp and dread,
In some god's reign, some god long fled.—
Thou gaseous puff of mineral breath
Mephitical ; thou swooning flaw
That fann'st me from this pond of death ;
Wert thou that venomous small thing
Which tickled with the poisoned straw ?
Thou, stronger, but who yet couldst start
Shrinking with sympathetic sting,
While willing the uncompunctious dart !
Ah, ghosts of Sodom, how ye thrill
About me in this peccant air,
Conjuring yet to spare, but spare !
Fie, fie, that didst in formal will
Plot piously the posthumous snare.
And thou, the mud-flow—evil mass

Of surest-footed sluggishness
Swamping the nobler breed—art there ?
Moan, burker of kind heart : all 's known
To Him ; with thy connivers, moan.—
Sinners—expelled, transmuted souls
Blown in these airs, or whirled in shoals
Of gurgles which your gasps send up,
Or on this crater marge and cup
Slavered in slime, or puffed in stench—
Not ever on the tavern bench
Ye lolled.   Few dicers here, few sots,
Few sluggards, and no idiots.
'Tis *thou* who servedst Mammon's hate
Or greed through forms which holy are—
Black slaver steering by a star,
'Tis *thou*—and all like thee in state.
Who knew the world, yet varnished it ;
Who traded on the coast of crime
Though landing not ; who did outwit
Justice, his brother, and the time—
These, chiefly these, to doom submit.
But who the manifold may tell ?
And sins there be inscrutable,
Unutterable.'
                    Ending there
He shrank, and like an osprey gray
Peered on the wave.   His hollow stare
Marked then some smaller bubbles play
In cluster silvery like spray :
' Be these the beads on the wives'-wine,
Tofana-brew ?—O fair Medea—
O soft man-eater, furry fine :
Oh, be thou Jael, be thou Leah—
Unfathomably shallow !—No !
Nearer the core than man can go

Or Science get—nearer the slime
Of Nature's rudiments and lime
In chyle before the bone.   Thee, thee,
In thee the filmy cell is spun—
The mould thou art of what men be :
Events are all in thee begun—
By thee, through thee !—Undo, undo,
Prithee, undo, and still renew
The fall forever ! '
                              On his throne
He lapsed ; and muffled came the moan
How multitudinous in sound,
From Sodom's wave.   He glanced around :
They all had left him, one by one.
Was it because he open threw
The inmost to the outward view ?
Or did but pain at frenzied thought
Prompt to avoid him, since but naught
In such case might remonstrance do ?
But none there ventured idle plea,
Weak sneer, or fraudful levity.

       Two spirits, hovering in remove,
Sad with inefficacious love,
Here sighed debate : ' Ah, Zoima, say ;
Be it far from me to impute a sin,
But may a sinless nature win
Those deeps he knows ? '—' Sin shuns that way ;
Sin acts the sin, but flees the thought
That sweeps the abyss that sin has wrought.
Innocent be the heart and true—
Howe'er it feed on bitter bread—
That, venturous through the Evil led,
Moves as along the ocean's bed
Amid the dragon's staring crew.'

XXXVII

OF TRADITIONS

CREDIT the Arab wizard lean,
And still at favouring hour are seen
(But not by Franks, whom doubts debar)
Through waves the cities overthrown :
Seboym and Segor, Aldemah,
With two whereof the foul renown
And syllables more widely reign.
     Astarte, worshipped on the Plain
Ere Terah's day, her vigil keeps
Devoted where her temple sleeps
Like moss within the agate's vein—
A ruin in the lucid sea.
The columns lie overlappingly—
Slant, as in order smooth they slid
Down the live slope.   Her ray can bid
Their beauty thrill along the lane
Of tremulous silver.   By the marge
(If yet the Arab credence gain)
At slack wave, when midsummer's glow
Widens the shallows, statues show—
He vouches ; and will more enlarge
On sculptured basins broad in span,
With alum scurfed and alkatran.
Nay, further—let who will, believe—
As monks aver, on holy eve,
Easter or John's, along the strand
Shadows Corinthian wiles inweave :
Voluptuous palaces expand,

From whose moon-lighted colonnade
Beckons Armida, deadly maid :
Traditions ; and their fountains run
Beyond King Nine and Babylon.
    But disenchanters grave maintain
That in the time ere Sodom's fall
'Twas shepherds here endured life's pain :
Shepherds, and all was pastoral
In Siddim ; Abraham and Lot,
Blanketed Bedouins of the plain ;
Sodom and her four daughters small—
For Sodom held maternal reign—
Poor little hamlets, such as dot
The mountain-side and valley way
Of Syria as she shows to-day ;
The East, where constancies indwell,
Such hint may give : 'tis plausible.

    Hereof the group—from Mortmain's blight
Withdrawn where sands the beach embayed
And Nehemiah apart was laid—
Held curious discourse that night.
They chatted ; but 'twas underrun
By heavier current. And anon,
After the meek one had retired
Under the tent, the thought transpired,
And Mortmain was the theme.
                             ' If mad,
'Tis indignation at the bad,'
Said Rolfe ; ' most men somehow get used
To seeing evil, though not all
They see ; 'tis sympathetical ;
But never some are disabused
Of first impressions which appal.'
    ' There, there,' cried Derwent, ' let it fall.

Assume that some are but so-so,
They 'll be transfigured.   Let suffice :
Dismas he dwells in Paradise.'
' Who ? '   ' Dismas the Good Thief, you know.
Ay, and the Blest One shared the cup
With Judas ; e'en let Judas sup
With Him, at the Last Supper too.—
But see ! '
    It was the busy Jew
With chemic lamp aflame, by tent
Trying some shrewd experiment
With minerals secured that day,
Dead unctuous stones.
      ' Look how his ray,'
Said Rolfe, ' too small for stars to heed,
Strange lights him, reason's sorcerer,
Poor Simon Magus run to seed.
And, yes, 'twas here—or else I err—
The legends claim, that into sea
The old magician flung his book
When life and lore he both forsook :
The evil spell yet lurks, may be.—
But yon strange orb—can be the moon ?
These vapours : and the waters swoon.'

  Ere long the tent received them all ;
They slumber—wait the morning's call.

XXXVIII

THE SLEEP-WALKER

Now Nehemiah with wistful heart
Much heed had given to myths which bore
Upon that Pentateuchal shore ;
Him could the wilder legend thrill
With credulous impulse, whose appeal,
Oblique, touched on his Christian vein.
Wakeful he bode. With throbbing brain
O'erwrought by travel, long he lay
In febrile musings, life's decay,
Begetting soon an ecstasy
Wherein he saw arcade and fane
And people moving in the deep ;
Strange hum he heard, and minstrel-sweep.
Then, by that sleight each dreamer knows,
Dream merged in dream : the city rose—
Shrouded, it went up from the wave ;
Transfigured came down out of heaven
Clad like a bride in splendour brave.
There, through the streets, with purling sound
Clear waters the clear agates lave,
Opal and pearl in pebbles strown ;
The palaces with palms were crowned—
The water-palaces each one ;
And from the fount of rivers shone
Soft rays as of Saint Martin's sun ;
Last, dearer than ere Jason found,
A fleece—the Fleece upon a throne !

And a great voice he hears which saith,
Pain is no more, no more is death ;
I wipe away all tears : Come, ye,
Enter, it is eternity.
And happy souls, the saved and blest,
Welcomed by angels and caressed,
Hand linked in hand like lovers sweet,
Festoons of tenderness complete—
Roamed up and on, by orchards fair
To bright ascents and mellower air ;
Thence, highest, toward the thone were led,
And kissed, amid the sobbings shed
Of faith fulfilled.—In magic play
So to the meek one in the dream
Appeared the New Jerusalem :
Haven for which how many a day—
In bed, afoot, or on the knee—
He yearned : Would God I were in thee !

The visions changed and counterchanged—
Blended and parted—distant ranged,
And beckoned, beckoned him away.
In sleep he rose ; and none did wist
When vanished this somnambulist.

XXXIX

THE camel's skull upon the beach
No more the sluggish waters reach—
No more the languid waters lave ;
Not now they wander in and out
Of those void chambers walled about—
So dull the calm, so dead the wave.
Above thick mist how pallid looms,
While the slurred day doth wanly break,
Ammon's long ridge beyond the lake.

Down to the shrouded margin comes
Lone Vine—and starts : not at the skull,
The camel's, for that bides the same
As when overnight 'twas Mortmain's stool.
But, nigh it—how *that* object name ?
Slant on the shore, ground-curls of mist
Enfold it, as in amethyst
Subdued, small flames in dead of night
Lick the dumb back-log ashy white.
What is it ?—paler than the pale
Pervading vapours, which so veil,
That some peak-tops are islanded
Baseless above the dull, dull bed
Of waters, which not e'en transmit
One ripple 'gainst the cheek of It.

327

The start which the discoverer gave
Was physical—scarce shocked the soul,
Since many a prior revery grave
Forearmed against alarm's control.
To him, indeed, each lapse and end
Meet—in harmonious method blend.
Lowly he murmured, ' Here is balm :
Repose is snowed upon repose—-
Sleep upon sleep ; it is the calm
And incantation of the close.'
The others, summoned to the spot,
Were staggered : Nehemiah ? no !
The innocent and sinless—what !—
Pale lying like the Assyrian low ?

The Swede stood by ; nor after-
        taste
Extinct was of the liquid waste
Nor influence of that Wormwood Star
Whereof he spake. All overcast—
His genial spirits meeting jar—
Derwent on no unfeeling plea
Held back. Mortmain, relentless : ' See :
To view death on the bed—at ease—
A dream, and draped ; to minister
To inheriting kin ; to comfort *these*
In chamber comfortable :—*here*
The elements all that unsay !
The first man dies. Thus Abel lay.'
The sad priest, rightly to be read
Scarce hoping—pained, dispirited—
Was dumb. And Mortmain went aside
In thrill by only Vine, espied :
Alas (thought Vine), thou bitter Swede,
Into thine armour dost thou bleed ?

Intent but poised, the Druze looked on :
' The sheath : the sword ? '
                              ' Ah, whither gone ? '
Clarel, and bowed him there and kneeled :
' Whither art gone ? thou friendliest mind
Unfriended—what friend now shalt find ?
Robin or raven, hath God a bird
To come and strew thee, lone interred,
With leaves, when here left far behind ? '
            ' He 's gone,' the Jew ; ' czars, stars
                must go
Or change ! All 's chemistry. Aye so.'—
' *Resurget* '—faintly Derwent there.
' *In pace* '—Vine, nor more would dare.

            Rolfe in his reaching heart did win
Prelude remote, yet gathering in :
' Moist, moist with sobs and balsam shed—
Warm tears, cold odours from the urn—
They hearsed in heathen Rome their dead
All hopeless of the soul's return.
Embracing them, in marble set,
The mimic gates of Orcus met—
The Pluto-bolt, the fatal one
Wreathed over by the hung festoon.
How fare we *now* ? But were it clear
In nature or in lore devout
That parted souls live on in cheer,
Gladness would be—shut pathos out.
His poor thin life : the end ? no more ?
The end here by the Dead Sea shore ? '
            He turned him, as awaiting nod
Or answer from earth, air, or skies ;
But be it ether or the clod,
The elements yield no replies.

Cross-legged on a cindery height,
Belex, the fatalist, smoked on.
Slow whiffs ; and then, ' It needs be done :
Come, beach the loins there, Bethlehemite.'—

Inside a hollow free from stone
With camel-ribs they scooped a trench ;
And Derwent, rallying from blench
Of Mortmain's brow, and nothing loath
Tacit to vindicate the cloth,
Craved they would bring to him the Book,
Now ownerless.   The same he took,
And thence had culled brief service meet,
But closed, reminded of the psalm
Heard when the salt fog shrunk the palm—
They wending toward these waters' seat—
Raised by the saint, as e'en it lent
A voice to low presentiment :
Naught better might one here repeat :
  ' *Though through the valley of the shade*
    I pass, no evil do I fear ;
  His candle shineth on my head :
    Lo, He is with me, even here.'

That o'er, they kneeled—with foreheads
  bare
Bowed as he made the burial prayer.
Even Margoth bent him ; but 'twas so
As some hard salt at sea will do
Holding the narrow plank that bears
The shotted hammock, while brief prayers
Are by the master read mid war
Relentless of wild elements—
The sleet congealing on the spar :
It was a sulking reverence.

The body now the Arabs placed
Within the grave, and then with haste
Had covered, but for Rolfe's restraint :
' The Book ! '—The Bible of the saint—
With that the relics there he graced,
Yea, put it in the hand : ' Since now
The last long journey thou dost go,
Why part thee from thy friend and guide !
And better guide who knoweth ?   Bide.'

They closed.   And came a rush, a roar—
Aloof, but growing more and more,
Nearer and nearer.   They invoke
The long Judaic range, the height
Of nearer mountains hid from sight
By the blind mist.   Nor spark nor smoke
Of that plunged wake their eyes might see ;
But, hoarse in hubbub, horribly,
With all its retinue around—
Flints, dust, and showers of splintered stone,
An avalanche of rock down tore,
In somerset from each rebound—
Thud upon thump—down, down and down—
And landed.   Lull.   Then shore to shore
Rolled the deep echo, fold on fold,
Which, so reverberated, bowled
And bowled far down the long El Ghor.

They turn ; and, in that silence sealed,
What works there from behind the veil ?
A counter-object is revealed—
A thing of heaven, and yet how frail :
Up in thin mist above the sea
Humid is formed, and noiselessly,
The fog-bow : segment of an oval

Set in a colourless removal
Against a vertical shaft, or slight
Slim pencil of an aqueous light.
Suspended there, the segment hung
Like to the May-wreath that is swung
Against the pole.   It showed half spent—
Hovered and trembled, paled away, and—went.

END OF PART II